Biblical Wisdom Literature
Part III

Father Joseph W. Koterski

THE TEACHING COMPANY ®

PUBLISHED BY:

THE TEACHING COMPANY
4840 Westfields Boulevard, Suite 500
Chantilly, Virginia 20151-2299
1-800-TEACH-12
Fax—703-378-3819
www.teach12.com

ISBN 1-59803-526-6

Father Joseph W. Koterski, Ph.D.

Associate Professor of Philosophy, Fordham University

Reverend Joseph W. Koterski, S.J., is a native of Cleveland, Ohio. He graduated from Xavier University (in Cincinnati, Ohio) with an Honors A.B. in Classical Languages and received his Ph.D. in Philosophy from St. Louis University with a dissertation entitled "The Dialectic of Truth and Freedom in the Philosophy of Karl Jaspers." He taught for several years at the University of St. Thomas (in Houston, Texas) and Loyola College (in Baltimore, Maryland). Since his priestly ordination in 1992, Father Koterski has been a member of the Philosophy department at Fordham University and was chair of that department from 2002 to 2005. At Fordham he also serves as the editor-in-chief of *International Philosophical Quarterly* and as master of Queen's Court Residential College for Freshmen.

Father Koterski's areas of special academic interest include ethics, metaphysics, and the history of medieval philosophy. He regularly teaches courses on natural law ethics and on medieval philosophy, and he has been awarded the Undergraduate Teaching Award (1998) and the Graduate Teacher of the Year Award (2000) at Fordham. For The Teaching Company, he has previously produced the courses *The "Ethics" of Aristotle* and *Natural Law and Human Nature*.

Father Koterski has delivered many scholarly and public lectures in the course of his career, including the Wethersfield Lectures sponsored by the Homeland Foundation in New York City and the Bradley Lecture at Belmont Abbey College. He is the author of some 70 scholarly articles and more than 200 book reviews. Since 1992, he has edited the annual proceedings of the University Faculty of Life, entitled *Life and Learning*, and has edited or coedited five books. Among his most recent publications is *An Introduction to Medieval Philosophy: Basic Concepts* (Wiley-Blackwell, 2008).

Table of Contents
Biblical Wisdom Literature
Part III

Credits

Biblical Wisdom Literature

Scope:

This course surveys biblical wisdom literature by a study of important scriptural texts, including Proverbs, Job, Qoheleth (Ecclesiastes), Sirach (Ecclesiasticus), Song of Songs (Canticle of Cancticles), Daniel, Wisdom of Solomon, and selections from the Gospels as well as from the book of Psalms.

The lectures take up the array of topics and problems that are recurrent in the Bible's sapiential books, with special emphasis on the problem of the suffering of the innocent but also including such themes as friendship, virtue and vice, marriage and the choice of a spouse, decision making, life priorities, child rearing, illness, and death.

Because the parts of scripture relevant to this course are especially sacred to Judaism and to Christianity, the approach taken here tries to be respectful both to the synagogue and to the church, for both revere this material and have sophisticated ideas about the Bible and its proper interpretation. They share a reverence for the Torah, for the Prophets, and for other writings such as the Psalms that are studied in this course. What Christianity recognizes as the New Testament stands in a profound continuity with what came before, whether we think of this as the Hebrew Bible or as the Old Testament (understood as a canon of scriptural texts that includes a few additional documents that are not in the Hebrew Bible but are nonetheless connected to the chosen people of Israel). In the New Testament there are various elements that stand within the wisdom tradition, such as some of the sayings and sermons of Jesus within the Gospels, and so these too are part of our study.

The lectures in this course regularly consider the place of the sapiential books within the Bible—they are in some respects different in kind from the other books of scripture but in many respects deeply connected to the rest. Although the books of biblical wisdom literature are not the historical record of God's people, they do touch on history from time to time, as when Sirach turns to the ranks of the patriarchs for inspirational examples of virtue or when Wisdom reflects on the plagues sent upon the Egyptians to illustrate the proactive role of divine providence. Although the books of biblical wisdom literature are not legal texts, they do regularly advert to the central biblical idea of covenant as essential to a life of wisdom, precisely because wisdom requires right relation to God and it is by the covenant that God has established the pattern for such right relationship. Although the books of biblical wisdom literature do not contain the type of magisterial pronouncements typical of the prophets, they do bear witness to the same concerns that engage the prophets, but with a more philosophical tenor in their way of addressing the pressing questions of how to live one's life, and they regularly return to the notion that the fear of the LORD is the beginning of wisdom.

Through a careful study of each of the sapiential books in turn, this course tries to show that the "wisdom" offered by the Bible refers to the understanding, the knowledge, the good sense, and the insight that comes ultimately from God but that is accessible to us in various ways, both by receiving the wisdom that God offers and by thinking things through for ourselves. The course suggests three primary forms of "wisdom": the wisdom that God would teach us; the wisdom that nature, cosmos, and creatures have to teach us; and the wisdom that is the result of human effort, that is the understanding of human nature and human behavior that arises from reflection on experience.

Because of the centrality of the notion of covenant in biblical theology, the course turns at a number of crucial places to a consideration of the historical record of divine initiatives in making a covenant with the chosen people and to a study of the theology of the covenant. This involves reflection on the biblical texts that deal with Adam and Eve, Noah, Abraham, Moses, David, Jeremiah, and Christ. In particular, the change made in the covenant at the time of Noah proves to be of special importance for understanding the problem of the suffering of the innocent.

A course such as this also needs to be attentive to various questions about the texts of scripture under study. For this reason, the lectures frequently take up issues of authorship, date of composition, textual problems, and the range of possible interpretations. The course tries to present the best of contemporary scholarship as well as a reverence for traditions of interpretation that have been prominent in various streams of thought within Judaism and Christianity.

While the course does not try to be a philosophy course, there are places where comparisons with certain philosophical ideas and schools of thought need to be discussed—on the problem of suffering raised by the book of Job and the relation of human suffering to God, for instance. This course also addresses some philosophical notions in the discussion of death and immortality in relation to sapiential books such as Wisdom of Solomon and the Gospels.

Finally, throughout the course, there is a consistent effort to call upon human experience, both the experience of the writers of these sapiential books and the experience of those listening to these lectures. One of the important senses of wisdom, after all, is the wisdom that is the fruit of human efforts to understand God, the world, and human nature. Accordingly, the lectures try to make this material accessible both for believers and nonbelievers, for those who are already adherents of the revealed religion and for those still searching. The material certainly lends itself to an open-ended reflection of this sort, for biblical wisdom literature often presses hard on life's important questions and tries to stretch the limits of our imaginations. The problem of suffering is a good example of this, for suffering can prompt deep questions of faith, especially when a person doubts the justice of God or suspects that there must be some guilt deep within as the reason for the suffering being experienced. This course tries to plumb the texts of biblical wisdom and to offer some important distinctions in order to clarify our thinking about these matters. It also tries to reflect on the value of prayer and on the virtue of compassion in accompanying those whose suffering we cannot alleviate.

Lecture Twenty-Five
Interlude—Wisdom Psalms on Perseverance

Scope:

This lecture will continue our practice of dipping from time to time into the treasury of the Psalter, this time to consider a number of psalms that are especially relevant for moments when perseverance is needed to counter delay and discouragement. The range of emotions and feelings that come to our attention in texts like the Song of Songs make this an opportune time to consider the role of prayer and wise guidance in the healing of injuries and in the right ordering of emotions.

Outline

I. Ordering our loves aright.

    A. By this point in our course, it is quite clear that the Bible's wisdom teaching is not of some abstract sort—it is frequently wisdom of heart as much as of head.

    B. To give one's love, heart and soul, to God as to a spouse, in the way that the Song of Songs suggests both literally and allegorically, requires a deep purity of heart. That notion—"purity of heart"—rings through the psalms and will echo in the wisdom teaching of the New Testament (e.g., in the Beatitudes).

II. Scriptural vocabulary.

    A. Because the Hebrew of the scriptures tends to be very concrete, translators face some important choices. If they aim for too literal a rendering of the text, we will be reading not just about "heart" but about "liver" and "loins" and any number of other internal organs. If they are too abstract or too free with their translations, we will miss half the point that it is through the body that we carry out the choices we make and that we express ourselves.

    B. In part, the problem that we face in understanding biblical terminology right is actually a philosophical problem. Ever since the beginning of the modern era, many Western languages and the cultural outlook that shapes them have come to reflect a certain dualism of mind and body.

C. The Bible takes an approach quite different from that of any dualist or materialist philosophy. Whether in the Creation story of Genesis or in the psalms that we will consider here, there is a strong sense of the unity of the material and the spiritual elements in each human being.

D. Interestingly, with the use of Greek terms like *psyche* (soul) as the translation of *nephesh* in the deuterocanonical (apocryphal) writings of the Old Testament as well as the whole of the New Testament, the shift in language will help to open up a crucial part of the Christian answer to the problem of suffering and death.

E. Here in the psalms we do well to ponder the ways in which the vocabulary of heart and liver and breath and life is used to express the inner depths of personal subjectivity as ways for expressing the self, the feelings, the emotions, and the inner core of the person.

III. Praying for purity of heart.

    A. Psalm 73 [72] opens with a strong sense of the difference between the "pure of heart" and "the proud" in a way that reminds us of the recurrent problem of wisdom literature.

    B. One of the aspects of biblical prayer that I personally find most helpful is the brutal honesty that it shows. Praying a psalm like this one summons us to speak the simple truth.

    C. I find that verses like these are very helpful in praying for genuine honesty in my examinations of conscience, especially if there is any hint of self-pity or feeling sorry for myself.

    D. The psalmist's first move is to make clear to himself during his prayer just how he is really feeling. Once what he is truly feeling gets expressed, he can see that there is something untoward. What exactly to do about it is not clear, and so he begs for the grace of God's light to penetrate the mystery.

    E. These lines tell both about one's conduct on earth and one's hope of heaven. They speak of God not just in an earthly way but as "my portion forever." They express a confidence that God will resolve the problems of present injustice and rectify wrong.

IV. A reflection on this kind of prayer.

    A. In praying this or any psalm, there is obviously no guarantee that one will feel what the psalmist is feeling or will experience the progress, the movement of spirit, that the psalmist is recording. Rather, the point is that the psalms are recognized to have God's sanction and approval as a way for us to pray.

    B. In a psalm like this one, the lesson for our prayer (it seems to me) might be to learn to pause, with the psalmist, and to reflect for as long as we need to.

    C. A psalm like this one gives us the encouragement to bring ourselves just as we are before the LORD. We may need some special grace to set our distorted loves back into right order or to make a good judgment in the presence of conflicting feelings.

    D. It seems to me that the psalmist must be someone who has been trained in the school of prayer—someone who knows how to wait and how to discern the difference between an untrustworthy feeling and a sound one, a fallacious line of reasoning and a true one.

    E. When we make an act of trust, it is not that we are always already feeling it but that we know we need to make that act of trust in God, and we hope that he will bring the feeling.

V. Application of the Song of Songs.

    A. I chose this psalm and this theme in light of the situation of the protagonist in the Song of Songs.

    B. The structure that I use begins with a prayer of gratitude to God for what the day has brought and a prayer of request for the light to see what God wants me to see.

    C. This is a spiritual exercise you might want to try the next time you find that you are "replaying the tape" of some difficult conversation or angry moment over and over again in the course of the day.

Suggested Reading:

Gallagher, *The Discernment of Spirits*.

Tournay, *Seeing and Hearing God with the Psalms*.

Questions to Consider:

1. What works best for you when you need to face something in prayer and find it easy to distract yourself and hard to stay focused?

2. What, if any, is the point of staying quiet, without speaking, in prayer, until at least the time you have decided to devote to prayer has passed? Many writers on prayer recommend this practice. What do you think?

3. The psalmist exemplifies the practice of acknowledging his feelings before he judges them and decides what to do about them. What works for you with respect to getting yourself an honest assessment of your feelings? By what standards should one decide how best to deal with them?

Lecture Twenty-Five—Transcript
Interlude—Wisdom Psalms on Perseverance

This lecture will continue our practice of dipping from time to time into the treasury of the psalter, this time to consider a number of psalms that are especially relevant for moments when perseverance is needed to counter delay and discouragement. The range of our emotions and feelings that come to our attention in texts like the Song of Songs that we were looking at in the last lecture, make this an opportune time to consider the role of prayer and wise guidance; for example, for healing of injuries or for the right ordering of our emotions.

Let's turn then to our subject, the importance of prayer for doing that. It is a task, I think, all our life long to try to order our loves aright because spontaneously we feel ourselves attracted, or on the other hand, revulsed by things and it's a question of getting our loves in sync with what the divine will is. By this point in the course, I think it is clear that the Bible's wisdom teaching is not of some abstract sort. Frequently, it is a wisdom of heart as much as a wisdom of head. I don't mean by this comment that it is simply a matter of following one's heart or one's feelings all the time. For the sapiential books of the Bible have made it clear that one's inclinations, one's desires, one's spontaneous attractions, can be badly ordered just as easily as they can be well ordered. To have rightly ordered loves, to have well-ordered desires, means that we need to use our head, our power of reason to figure out what that right order of love is and then to try to bring our own emotions and desires in sync with that. We may well need to work quite hard at reigning in certain feelings and emotions as well as giving others free play so as to have a rightly ordered heart.

To give one's love, heart, and soul to God as to a spouse, in the way that the Song of Songs for instance, suggests, both at the literal level and at the allegorical level, requires a deep purity of heart. That notion, "purity of heart," rings through the Psalms and will echo also in the teaching of the New Testament. For instance, it has a tremendously important place in the Beatitudes, but what does it mean and how are we to get purity of heart? To answer this question, let me suggest that we turn our attention, as we have done several times during this course, to some of the psalms, and in this way to reinforce the connection between wisdom and prayer.

I'd like to begin our discussion of that topic by looking at the question of the vocabulary that scripture uses. As we prepare to enter into some of the psalms that deal with human affections and human feelings, it may be helpful to recall some of these things about the terminology both in our translations and in the original Hebrew. Their way of understanding the makeup of a human person is distinctive. Because the Hebrew of the scriptures tends to be so very concrete, translators face important choices here. If they aim for too literal a rendering of the text, we will be reading not just about the heart but about the liver and the loins and any number of other internal organs. That's the actual words that are used in the Hebrew text. On the other hand, if the translators get too abstract or too free with their translations of these terms, we could easily miss half the point, that it is through the body that we carry out the choices that we make and that we express ourselves.

In part, the problem that we face in understanding biblical terminology correctly is actually a philosophical problem. In the modern era in which we live, ever since the beginning of that period, many Western languages and the cultural outlook that helps shape and are shaped by these languages, have come to reflect a certain dualism of mind and body. Descartes, for example, creator of analytic geometry and a famous philosopher in his own right, talked about a great split between body and soul. He spoke about body as what is extended in spatial dimensions, whereas he regarded mind or soul as unextended. This was thinking stuff as opposed to extended stuff. But that's a pretty strong split and he had a very difficult time putting body and soul together and explaining how they interacted. Likewise, the great German philosopher of the Enlightenment period, Emmanuel Kant, differentiated between the phenomenal world of appearances in space and time, and the noumenal world of mind and idea which had no spatial dimension. That too is a kind of split which he tried to put together, and maybe not quite so successfully in my point of view, but even apart from its philosophical validity, both of the ideas have this great split between body and soul.

While dualist philosophers have considerable trouble explaining how anything material can act upon anything spiritual and vice versa, materialist philosophers of our age, and there are plenty of those, have denied the need to grant the reality of anything spiritual or immaterial. Their views tend to reduce even our thinking and willing and choosing to the physical, to the realm of the bodily, despite their inability to account for how meaning works as well as how freedom of choice works. I think that there are better philosophical approaches that we could use but that is not our direct concern here. Rather, what we want to do is to understand the biblical view and to do so we need to be aware of the fact that sometimes the prevailing terminology and the prevailing mindset in our culture may obscure what the Bible has in mind.

The Bible takes an approach quite different from any dualist or any materialist philosophy. Whether we're back in the creation story of Genesis or in the Psalms that we'll be considering in this lecture, there is a strong sense of the unity of the material and the spiritual elements in each human being. To use the language of Genesis, the human being is made from the "dust of the earth" and animated by God's "life-giving spirit" and they have a sense that there's just a great unity to that human person. You've got to deal with both the material and the spiritual aspects in order to get it right.

The concrete vocabulary of the scriptures helps to teach that lesson by using words like heart, in Hebrew, *lev*, for the center of the person and using the word for hands, singular is *yad* or plural *yamin*, for a person's actions. The word that's often translated as soul in some Bible translations that we will be using, you may use privately, that word is *nephesh*, whose more than 750 appearances in the scriptures make it clear that it refers to anything living, anything that is animated, both to plants and animals as well as to human beings. There's a life character to it. It does not refer to this separate immaterial substance that the dualist philosophies had proposed.

Interestingly, with the use of Greek terms—because of course the Old Testament was translated into Greek called the Septuagint and then the New Testament is written in Greek, with the use of Greek terms like *psychē*, the origin of our word psychological, which means, in Greek, soul or life principle, as a translation of the Hebrew term, *nephesh*, this notion of life as the Hebrew language expresses it—the use of these Greek terms in the deutero-canonical writings or for some translations the apocryphal writings of the Old Testament, as well as in the whole of the New Testament, there is a shift in language here that will help us to understand and open up a crucial part of the Christian answer to the problem of suffering and death. Namely, the Greek language is accustomed to having words for soul that make it easy to talk about immortality of the soul and also to talk about resurrection of the body and yet to preserve this basic biblical insight that the whole person is a unity of body and soul. Even if there is an immortal soul that is separated from the body at death, it's not the complete person until we have again this resurrection of the body. We'll be seeing that when we turn to the Wisdom of Solomon as well as the text we study from the New Testament.

Here in the Psalms, we do well to ponder the ways in which there's simply a unified vocabulary suggested by these very concrete terms, terms for heart and liver and breath and life. All these terms are used to express both our bodily dimension but also the inner depths of personal subjectivity. These are ways for expressing the self, the feelings, the emotions, the inner core of the person.

Let's turn now to one of those psalms that I think will be very useful and helpful for us to study in this part of our course, namely, Psalm 73, which is, I think, about praying for purity of heart. The psalm opens with a strong sense of the difference between those who are "pure of heart" and "the proud." That's an interesting sort of contrast to make. We might think of pride as in the head and heart as somehow here in our desires. They're contrasting "pure of heart" and "proud" in a way that reminds us of that recurrent problem of wisdom literature, the need to make some good choices. Let me read from the beginning of that psalm here, first three verses:

> Truly God is good to Israel,
> To such as are pure of heart.
> But as for me, my feet had almost stumbled;
> My steps had nearly slipped.
> For I was envious of the boastful,
> When I saw the prosperity of the wicked.

It is not just that there is a question here of understanding why the wicked prosper and the innocent suffer, that was the issue that we saw raised in Job and Qoheleth, but an acknowledgment of the feelings that are involved, for instance, in a person who's trying to be good and yet knows that there's a temptation to do otherwise. The person here, I think, is acknowledging a feeling of being envious, of being tempted to switch sides by abandoning the discipline of Torah, by abandoning the patterns of wisdom that were taught by this very traditional education that someone who has been through Proverbs and Sirach has received.

One of the aspects of biblical prayer that I find most helpful personally and it's exhibited, I think, in a psalm like 73, is this blunt and brutal honesty that it shows. How many times have I found myself—maybe you as well—how many times do we find ourselves inclined to cover up the truth, inclined to rationalize in one way or another about our affairs? Oh no, it wasn't really like that. Well, praying a psalm like this one, summons us to speak the simple truth. Here is indeed how I felt. Here's what I was thinking about, and I think what the psalm is going to be suggesting for us is, God knows it anyway. So why—we can't deceive him—so why even try to deceive ourselves about it?

After several more verses about how well-off the wicked seem to have it, "no pains," bodies that are "sound and sleek," "no share in men's sorrows," with hearts that "overflow with malice" and minds that "seethe with plots," all those things are mentioned in verses 4–7, the psalmist then frankly admits how strong the temptation there is to join them.

> Therefore his people return here,
> And waters of a full cup are drained by them.
> And they say, "How does God know?
> And is there knowledge in the Most High?"
> Surely I have cleansed my heart in vain,
> And washed my hands in innocence,
> For all day long I have been plagued,
> And chastened every morning.

It's that honesty, knowing that there are feelings of the inclination to abandon all the harder routes, to abandon this stiffer climb that the roads of discipline and wisdom might encourage. I find that verses like these are very helpful in praying for genuine honesty. They're useful to me when I'm just praying them and I happen to run into this psalm or when I'm trying to make an examination of conscience. This is one of the psalms to which I like to turn, particularly because there is this sense of honesty to which the psalmist is himself trying to reach and which I find myself desirous of, especially if I'm feeling any hint of self-pity or feeling sorry for myself, one of those "poor me" sort of days. At least in my case there can be strong feelings in a certain direction that need to be exposed to the light. Maybe they are sound feelings, maybe they're unsound feelings, but until I advert to them, until I acknowledge what they are, there's no way to examine them and to judge them. I think that's what our psalmist is feeling.

Let's turn to the next few verses there. I'm now up to verses 15–17.

> If I had said, "I will speak thus,"
> Behold, I would have been untrue to the generation of Your
>   children,
> When I thought how to understand this,
> It was too painful for me—
> Until I went into the sanctuary of God;
> Then I understood their end.

I take those last lines to mean he was feeling the confusion and until he had recourse to prayer—he speaks of going into the sanctuary, perhaps going to a place of prayer and getting that different perspective realizing—what would be the end, what would be the result if he had followed out that feeling to which he was so inclined. There's a way in which he's feeling pulled in both directions and he needs to submit those feelings in quite considerable clarity about what they are, to the test of, does this match with the Torah, does this match with the discipline that he's learned?

The psalmist's first move then is to make clear to himself here during his prayer just how he is really feeling. Once what he is truly feeling gets expressed, he can see that there is something untoward about that particular feeling that he had. It could equally well have been that it was a good and sound one that he should stay with. So here, in this case, because there's something untoward, he turns and he can act on it. He begs God for the grace of light to penetrate this mystery. The next move that he makes is something very much in the spirit of what the wisdom literature calls the fear of the LORD. Again, not a servile fear, as we've said before, not somebody who's just afraid of getting punished, but a mature reverence for God's justice and mercy all at once. He really does, in his heart of hearts and his better self, want to stand with the LORD but he needs to let that indeed wash over him and feel it strongly so that he can make the right judgment. At verses 18 and 19:

> Surely You set them in slippery places;
> You cast them down to destruction.
> Oh, how they are brought to desolation, as in a moment!
> They are utterly consumed with terrors.

This consideration of what happens to those who make the wrong choice help the psalmist to remember the lessons of the wisdom literature in order to get the needed perspective. He continues, I'll read here at verse 21:

> Thus my heart was grieved,
> And I was vexed in my mind.
> I was so foolish and ignorant;
> I was like a beast before You.
> Never the less I am continually with You;
> You hold me by my right hand.
> You will guide me with Your counsel,
> And afterward receive me to glory.

I take that to be a comment on the change in the inner state and the inner sentiments that the psalmist is expressing. You know how hard it is even to record all the many things that go through our mind. When I think in literature of what authors do it, curiously someone like James Joyce has a wonderful way in his stream of consciousness techniques for trying to even write down all the many things that go through his mind. The psalmist doesn't ever achieve that stream of consciousness technique, but he does manage to convey, here in the form of a prayer, acknowledging some of the things he's going through. In the last few lines of the psalm, we get a strong sense of God's grace and direct assistance to him. The psalm concludes in a note of trust and confidence:

> Whom have I in heaven but You?
> And there is none upon earth that I desire besides You.
> My flesh and my heart fail;
> But God is the strength of my heart and my portion forever.
> For indeed, those who are far from You shall perish;
> You have destroyed all those who desert You for harlotry.
> But it is good for me to draw near to God;
> I have put my; trust in the LORD God,
> That I may declare all Your works.

These lines tell both about one's conduct on earth and one's hope of heaven. They speak of God not just in an earthly way or experienced here on earth, but as "my portion forever," not something that stops at death. They express a confidence that God will resolve the problems of present injustice and will rectify wrong and the final line is, quite rightly I think, an expression of thanks. Not that the word is used, but that the psalmist promises to tell what God does for him and that's a way of expressing thanks.

Let's now try to reflect on this kind of prayer that we've just examined in this particular psalm. In praying this psalm or any psalm, there is obviously no guarantee at all that one will feel exactly or even remotely what the psalmist is feeling or what the psalmist is writing about nor is there any guarantee that we'll experience the progress that I believe the psalmist shows as he went through that particular prayer, namely, the movement of spirit that this particular psalmist is recording. I do not believe that there is any way to mechanize one's prayers. The computer age will never touch them even if the computer gives us a way, perhaps, to read the psalms on screen.

Rather, the point is that the psalms are recognized to have God's sanction, God's approval. They are a good way for us to pray and they can help us to move in our feelings and to move in our sentiments even as they can help us to move in our thinking. They give us a good, solid reliable way of addressing God when the words may come hard to us or where we don't exactly how to proceed.

As in the some of the previous lectures that I gave on prayer, I'd like to make this point here: the goal is not to get to the end of the text. Here, we read through the whole of Psalm 73, but unless we're praying communally with others, and then we have to keep up the pace, the goal is not to get to the end of the text. Rather, the goal, especially when we're praying the psalms or some other passage by ourselves, the goal is to let the words speak to us, to give God the chance to address us and to raise our minds and hearts to God and to say what we need to say. I don't, in any way, begrudge a prayer if I even get only halfway through, if some real praying occurred, either some real listening or some real speaking.

In a psalm like this one, the lesson for our prayer, it seems to me, might be to learn to pause, just as the psalmist, I presume is pausing when he writes this and to reflect for as long as we need to do so on the first element in the strategy and then the second element that the psalmist proposes and then the third. For instance, are we feeling some of the self-pity at the good fortunes of others that, here, the psalmist notes in himself or are perhaps, we just confused about it? Are we feeling the anxiety that the bride in the middle of the night twice experienced in the Song of Songs that we looked at in the last lecture? Or just what is it that we feel?

Part of what I'm suggesting here is that that bride in the Song of Songs was so quick to rush out in her search. Fortunately she met her bridegroom the first time, even when the police didn't know where he was. The second time she never did find him outside, she only received a beating from the night wardens. Part of what we have to do if it's the time of panic or a time of self-pity, a time of uncertainty, or a time of some other strong feeling, who knows what it is, is that there's a need to wait in patience and perhaps to turn in prayer. A psalm like this one gives us the encouragement to bring ourselves just as we are before the LORD. Granted, God already knows our situation, but we may not yet fully grasp it. It's nice to have good vocabulary for our emotions but few of us have an adequate vocabulary for the things we're feeling and we may not even realize what we're feeling. God already knows what is there and God already knows whether we have or whether we lack the purity of heart that the psalmist mentions. Whether we have the right order of loves or whether the love map that we're using is a little bit disorganized or disordered, we may need some special help, some special grace to set our disordered loves or our uncertainties back into the right order. We may need some help to make good judgment in the presence of conflicting feelings.

I do not picture the psalm we were just reading there as something in which the psalmist is simply marching through a psalm like this from beginning to end. His words at verses 16 and following about finding the problem too hard to fathom, suggests to me that he was perplexed, that he found his feelings moving in opposite directions and that his memory of the wisdom teaching and the feelings were going against one another. But what he does in the prayer that is here recorded is to beg for God's help, better to understand. He begs for God's assistance, better to remember the wisdom that he has already learned in calmer and simpler times. He doesn't hide the fact that his heart sometimes grows embittered. He doesn't hide the fact that he feels stupid and cut to the quick, but it seems to me that what the psalmist does is rely upon the way in which he's already been trained. In this particular case, he has been trained in a sort of tradition, in a school of prayer and one of the things that we can cultivate in ourselves if we want to also grow in that school of prayer, is to learn how to wait, to learn how to discern the difference between a trustworthy and an untrustworthy feeling, a sound one in line of reasoning or a fallacious line of reasoning. The one who knows how to use a meditation like this can get back to the needed perspective. It lets us make an act of trust when we need to and trust, of course, means assuming that someone will be there to catch us, in this case the LORD himself. This is a venerable tradition in prayer. When we make an act of trust, it is not that we're already feeling it. Sometimes we have to say the words, "LORD I trust you" even when we know that what we've got to do is hope in him that he will even bring the feeling. All we can do with our mind is to say, "We trust you, we're relying upon you." There are many ways in which this can work. We'll see one of them, a very interesting case of trust, in the person of Daniel, when we turn to that as the next unit of biblical wisdom literature that we study in the next lecture.

What I'd like to do though is, for a moment, continue this reflection here with you by looking at what we just did from Psalm 73, applied to the Song of Songs. I chose this particular psalm and this theme in light of the situation of the protagonist of the Song of Songs; namely, that bride who found herself, very, very stirred and attracted. She wanted her bridegroom with her and yet, twice in the course of that particular text, she finds that he's gone and she's just very upset. If we confine ourselves for the moment to the plain sense of the text, there are those two moments of panic that set her off into this blind chase looking for her love in the wrong places. There probably are some appropriate allegorical levels about this for Israel and the Church and we looked at those a little bit in the last lecture.

There is an understandable desire to be loved in her, but it leads to a foolish action and what I mean by that is that in our human psychology, we're made both to give love and to receive it. So there's no denying, in fact we want to affirm, that she's feeling this need to both receive love and to give love aright. What the wisdom literature and what the Psalms have to say about that is found in any number of places. In Sirach for instance, Sirach had urged that the disciplines of Torah be used for learning how to give love and how to receive it. The psalm that we are treating here provides an equally important and indispensable aspect, real prayer, where Sirach had urged a kind of virtue, training by repetition, getting our mind straight so that our hearts would follow. The psalmist agrees with that but also urges that we pray when we get in those situations, and that we pray in all honesty before God and ourselves with genuine trust and also with a simple request to him that it need not be expressed in complicated words but simply put forth very directly. I find that when I'm trying to pray in that sort of situation, part of what I need to do is to slow down and say to the LORD, in so many words, "What is it that I'm seeking?" I need to voice the grace or the help that I'm asking for.

In my own practice of trying to make a daily examination of conscience, this is also a crucial part. The structure that I use when I'm trying to do this in light of a psalm like 73, I begin with a little prayer of gratitude to God for what the day has brought and then I request the light to see what it is God wants me to see. Usually those things go fairly quickly, and then I try to make a mental review of the actions and attitudes that have constituted the day. After I've done that for say, five or 10 minutes, going through the day, going through the tape as it were, then I try to make a resolution about what I want to do the following day, whether I want to continue on the same course or perhaps if I wandered off course, if I've got to change course and correct it. But then the final portion of this examination of conscience and I get it in line, I think, with psalms like 73, is that there's a need to ask for divine help to carry out whatever course I charted.

I think that this step is just so crucial for, you know, we can make our resolutions but often the resolutions we make may mean acting against some deeply established habit. And that means, yes, using my full willpower, but also asking for the help to have that habit, if it's a bad habit, be loosened and broken up. Or if it's the matter of the lack of a habit, for a better habit to be formed. Here's a spiritual exercise that you might want to try in light of this. The next time that you find yourself in one of those days when you're just, you've been troubled by something, like the psalmist has been troubled, and perhaps you have just gotten so angry—let's suppose the situation is you're replaying the tape so often just because you've been angry with somebody—the suggestion that you might want to try is this: eject the tape from your mind. It doesn't help to keep replaying it. At least what I find is that if I keep replaying it, I keep getting better and better and the other guy keeps getting worse and worse and that's not honest. Eject the tape, send it to the dead letter office by express mail, but promise yourself that when a moment of quiet comes that you can make a prayerful examination of conscience, then you'll look at the tape. You'll look at it with the hope of getting a little bit more objectivity, and when you get that greater objectivity and greater truthfulness, instead of increasing the anger or the emotion, one can replay the tape and do it, asking for divine help even to see what the situation really was.

So the exercise you might think of doing is see, does this help you to get closer to the truth or what is the experience for you? Are you, in replaying the tape, distorting the matter in your own favor? What Psalm 73 suggests to us is the need to pray in this regard and ask the LORD to help give us purity of heart, to help order our loves aright. We'll take a look at this in another biblical way by looking at the book of Daniel in our next lecture.

Lecture Twenty-Six
Daniel—Wisdom through Dream Visions

Scope:

The book of Daniel is clearly one of the later books of the Hebrew Bible (2nd century B.C.) and is sometimes classified with the prophetic books, but it warrants inclusion here by virtue of its dream visions, which can rightly be considered as a special kind of wisdom. This lecture will consider the question of its historical context and likely date as well as the textual problems that arise from the inclusion of certain passages in the deuterocanonical version that are regarded as apocryphal in the Jewish canon, such as the psalm of Azariah, the canticle of the three young men, the story of Susanna, and the satires on idolatry. After providing a general orientation to the book as a whole, the lecture will concentrate on the dream visions given to Daniel in chapters 1–6 as especially germane to the wisdom tradition.

Outline

I. Why consider Daniel a wisdom book?

    A. Earlier in this course we took note of the various approaches to wisdom in the Bible, and in the book of Daniel we find yet another kind.

    B. In Daniel we find an approach to wisdom through dreams and visions. One might call it a kind of prophetic wisdom, an insight that comes from divine revelation through the discernment of signs that are given in sleep and in contemplation.

II. The Bible and dreams.

    A. While books like Sirach generally warn against putting one's stock in dreams, Sirach does make an exception for dreams sent by God.

    B. In addition to the provision made for an authentic vision in the lines just quoted from Sirach, there is also the favorable outlook on dreams and visions in Joel and the interesting precedent for the possibility of reliable dream interpretation in the case of Joseph in Genesis.

C. The text of Daniel presents Daniel and his three companions as blessed by God with wisdom, and both the Jewish and Christian traditions have accepted Daniel within their canons.

III. General orientation to the book.

   A. The book has two parts: six chapters with edifying stories about Daniel as a model of heroic virtue, and then six chapters of his visions of God's providential plans for history.

   B. There are also some additional chapters that appear in the deuterocanonical (apocryphal) version that contain additional stories of virtuous heroism that make an important contribution to the wisdom character of the book by showing a very wise Daniel.

   C. The middle portion of the book is in the Aramaic language, with the beginning and the subsequent sections in Hebrew; from chapter 13 on, the text is available only in Greek.

   D. For this book and the remainder of the Old Testament passages, I will make use of the Revised Standard Version of the Bible.

IV. The historical context of the book's composition.

   A. As we saw in our discussion of Sirach, the rivalry between the generals who succeeded Alexander the Great (Ptolemy in Egypt and Seleucus in Syria, Babylon, and Persia) included competition for Palestine until Pompey conquered the entire region in 63 B.C.

   B. While the Ptolemies still controlled Palestine during the 3rd century B.C., larger numbers of Jews actually lived in the Diaspora than in Palestine, including many who came to Alexandria, where the Septuagint translation of the Bible was made.

   C. By 167 B.C., the office of the high priest had been seized, pagan worship had begun, and through the use of Hellenistic gymnasia there was pressure on Jewish youth to be ashamed of such customs as circumcision.

D. Antiochus desecrated the temple, confiscated sacred vessels, and then set up an altar to Olympian Zeus within the temple. He made Jewish religious practice a crime of treason and required the local authorities to accept the notion that the God of Israel was identical to the Greek Zeus, with Antiochus himself as his earthly regent.

E. Some aristocrats adapted themselves to Greek ways, but others resisted. Some resisted violently, while others encouraged resistance without violence.

V. The historical setting of the book.

A. The story recounted in Daniel comes not from the time of Antiochus but from the time of Israel's previous great crisis, the beginning of the exile from the southern kingdom of Judah at the moment of its collapse.

B. Setting the stories of Daniel during the Babylonian exile at the courts of Nebuchadnezzar, Belshazzar, and Darius testifies to the fact that troubles of this sort had happened before and that God could be trusted to provide courage in the face of persecution, and wisdom when specially needed.

VI. The wisdom elements in the book of Daniel.

A. The opening description of Daniel and his friends stresses their training in wisdom and their refusal to be corrupted by foreign wisdom.

B. When the sages whom Nebuchadnezzar commanded to interpret some dreams that had troubled him prove unable to do so, he threatens all his wise men with death.

C. When Daniel then interprets the image, Nebuchadnezzar appoints Daniel and his friends to positions of honor and rule.

D. Those jealous of their positions reveal that Daniel's three companions have refused to worship Nebuchadnezzar's golden statue. He has them cast into a fire heated seven times more than usual, and yet they—plus a mysterious fourth one who is "like a son of the gods" (3:25)—remain unburned. Nebuchadnezzar chalks this up to the protection of their own God (3:28) and frees them.

E. The final episode recounted here is the one in which Daniel is thrown into the lion pit for daring to pray to his God. His miraculous deliverance from death elicits a prayer of faith from King Darius and allows Daniel to prosper into the year of Cyrus.

VII. Wisdom in dreams.

   A. It is not merely Freudian psychology that has seen significance in dreams. The ancient world also had a profound sense of the importance of dreams.

   B. The text of Daniel turns next to Daniel's own dreams and visions, and we will follow the text in our next lecture, where we will also reflect further on Daniel as a wisdom book.

Suggested Reading:

Collins, *Daniel.*

Goldingay, *Daniel.*

The Holy Bible: Revised Standard Version, book of Daniel.

Questions to Consider:

1. What was the "abomination of desolation"? Why did it so appall the author?

2. What do you regard as the main point of the stories in the first section of Daniel?

3. Can there be wisdom in dreams and in stories about dream interpretations? What would you say to the objection that this is "just another story"?

Lecture Twenty-Six—Transcript
Daniel—Wisdom through Dream Visions

The book of Daniel is clearly one of the later books of the Hebrew Bible; it comes from the 2nd century B.C. In the printed versions of the Bible, it is sometimes classified with the prophetic books. But it warrants inclusion here in our study of wisdom literature especially because of the presence of dream visions which are described, and I think rightly considered, as a special kind of wisdom. This lecture will consider the question of the historical context of this book, the likely date of its composition, as well as some of the textual problems that arise from the inclusion of certain passages in the deuterocanonical version that are regarded as apocryphal in the Jewish canon, such as the psalm of Azariah, the canticle of the three young men, the story of Susanna, the satires on idolatry. After providing a general orientation to the book as a whole, this lecture will concentrate on those dream visions that are given to Daniel in chapters 1–6, because of the way in which they're especially germane to the wisdom tradition.

Why consider Daniel a wisdom book rather than say, a prophetic book? It doesn't merit classification under both schemes and it's often printed among the prophets. The wisdom that comes from divine inspiration can come in dreams. Earlier in the course, we took note of various approaches to receiving wisdom. The book of Daniel was yet another way of receiving it. There were books such as the book of Proverbs and the book of Sirach that teach wisdom about ordinary life through these maxims and sayings which a person is supposed to learn; learn by heart, commit to memory. Both books, the book of Sirach, the book of Proverbs, stay closely connected throughout to the careful study of Torah; wisdom comes from Torah.

Another tradition that we saw was present in books such as Job and Qoheleth, in a way that tends toward a philosophical kind of wisdom by the way in which the speakers press the questions about suffering and justice and meaning in life and they really do force the debate. Likewise, the Song of Songs, maybe not philosophical, but it also takes that version of drama as a way in which to seek wisdom precisely through telling a story and through dialogue.

In the book of Daniel, we find an approach to wisdom that uses a story and uses a narrative but the specific wisdom element comes through dreams and visions. One might call this, perhaps, a sort of prophetic wisdom, an insight that comes from a divine revelation through the discernment of the signs that are given, this time given in sleep as well as given in contemplation. It's important for us, I think, to consider the question about dreams and the Bible.

While books like Sirach had generally warned against putting one's stock in dreams, there are exceptions. Let me turn to a passage, going back to Sirach for a minute, chapter 34, the first eight verses, in which Sirach, himself, contemplates the prospect of getting wisdom from God in a dream:

> Empty and false are the hopes of the senseless,
>> and fools are borne aloft by dreams.
> Like a man who catches at shadows or chases the wind,
>> is the one who believes in dreams....
> Divination, omens and dreams are all unreal;
>> what you already expect, the mind depicts.
> Unless it be a vision specially sent by the Most High,
>> fix not your heart on it... (NAB: 34:1–2, 5–6)

We have there, clearly, in the book of Sirach, a sense that most dreams, most of these things should not be taken as coming from the LORD. Hence, Sirach is following very closely the sort of counsel that is prescribed earlier on in the Bible yet. In Deuteronomy 13:2–6, that passage very, very severely prescribes death for one who tries to lead others to idolatry on the basis of some dream. Likewise, in another one of the prophets, in Jeremiah at chapter 23, again at chapter 27, and a third time at chapter 29, Jeremiah labors to distinguish between true prophecy coming from God and false prophecies which he thinks generally come in dreams, however pious they seem. What Jeremiah is clearly doing is distinguishing between something that looks good if it comes in a dream and those relatively rare instances when it truly is from God; but how do you tell?

In addition to the provision that is made for the possibility of an authentic vision in the lines that I just quoted from Sirach, there are other passages in the Bible that are more favorable in their outlook on the possibility of dreams and visions coming from God, the prophet Joel, for instance; that's at chapter 2, verse 28. Likewise, there is the interesting precedent for the possibility of reliable dream interpretation that comes in Genesis when the figure, the patriarch Joseph, has to interpret the dreams of Pharaoh; that's in chapter 37 and chapter 40. Joseph is first given a dream himself about his own relationship to his brothers and then is later given this ability to interpret the dreams that Pharaoh has. In this, it's clearly from God, as well as the interpretation, clearly from God. It's a kind of wisdom.

The question is not whether God might communicate in oracles and in visions or in dreams, for so many prophets have experienced God in visions, but rather, whether any given vision is authentically from God or not. There were many false prophets in Israel and much of the story about the prophets is a matter of discerning a true prophet from a false prophet. It's a question of knowing when to accept a vision as part of the tradition of wisdom or on the other hand, regard it as something false. Within the wisdom tradition, much of which proceeds didactically through Proverbs and philosophically through story and drama, this can give yet another access to divine wisdom when it's handled carefully.

The text of Daniel presents a young man, Daniel, and his three companions especially blessed by God with wisdom. Both the Jewish and the Christian traditions have accepted Daniel within their canons. So the book is canonical, although there will be some chapters, we'll get to it, which one tradition regards as apocryphal, the other tradition regards as canonical, or perhaps in a technical sense, deuterocanonical; both of them accept the book in general. Let's listen to the very first line of this:

> As for these four youths, God gave them learning and skill in all letters and wisdom; and Daniel had understanding in all visions and dreams. (1:17)

There's the book talking about this divine precedent, this divine authority for what Daniel experienced. There's also an important point to consider from biblical history. As we will see in more detail when we consider the historical context of this particular book, the book has a foreign setting and the foreign setting of the story not only has bearing on God's providential care for Israel but it also, I think, is designed to show the superiority of Israel's wisdom to the claimed wisdom of surrounding nations, for instance, when God gives Daniel and his three friends an understanding that is so far superior to that of foreign kings and their wise men. One sees this in the first chapter, verse 4, or verses 17–20, but one will see it again repeatedly in this first half of the book. The whole of chapter 2 in a way is about that; from the very end of chapter 3 at verse 31 to chapter 4, verse 34, and then yet again in chapter 5 for the verses between 11 and 14. There's that contrast between the kind of wisdom that these foreign cultures have and the superior wisdom that God has provided for wise men like Daniel and his friends that are in the tradition of Israel.

It will pay us now to do a general orientation to the book, looking first at its structure. The book has two parts; six chapters, the first six, deal with edifying stories about Daniel as a model of heroic virtue. The next six chapters deal with the visions that Daniel receives for God's providential plan for history, for the outcome for Israel. There are also some additional chapters that appear in the deuterocanonical or apocryphal version that contain additional stories. They are stories about virtuous heroism and they make an important contribution to the wisdom character of the book by showing a very wise Daniel as he exhibits the wisdom of judgment, a judgment like that of King Solomon.

This is part of the textual problem. The middle portion of the book, from chapter 2, verse 4, the second half of that verse, all the way through chapter 7, verse 28, the book is in Aramaic and not in Hebrew. The beginning section of the book, from chapter1, verse 1, up to chapter 2, verse 4 and then from chapter 8, verse 1 to chapter 12, verse 13, that is in Hebrew. From chapter 13 on, the only text we have is in Greek and not only that it's in Greek, but there are two versions in Greek. So the textual problems are considerable here.

For this book and for the remainder of the Old Testament passages that I will be citing, I'll make use of the Revised Standard Version of the Bible. This is a very reliable translation. It is a revision of what was called the American Standard Version that had been published in 1901 and that in turn, is a revision of the original King James Version. So the translation history here has a very, very fine and noble pedigree.

The historical context for this book's composition—as we saw in our discussion of the book of Sirach—the historical situation here is complex. There's a rivalry, in this case, between the generals who succeeded Alexander the Great, Ptolemy in Egypt, Seleucus over in Syria, Babylon and Persia and they're competing for various lands, including competing for Palestine. This competition between their descendants continues until finally the Roman General, Pompey, conquers the entire region in the year 63 B.C.

While the Ptolemies still controlled Palestine during the 3rd century B.C., there were a larger number of Jews who lived in Diaspora than lived in Palestine. Diaspora is when the Jewish community had to spread out and lived in various lands. Many of them came to Alexandria and it was in Alexandria that the Greek translation of the Bible was made, the one that's called the Septuagint. Not long after 200 B.C. the Seleucids took control of Palestine. The prospect of greater religious freedom under the Seleucids initially delighted the Jewish population of Jerusalem, but then, this prospect of more freedom was quickly disappointed with the rise of a ruler by the name of Antiochus IV Epiphanes. He ruled from 175 B.C. to 164 B.C. and his policy of the forcible Hellenization of Jerusalem, that was a very tremendous challenge. There's also the problem that the community faced because of the cooperation in this program of Hellenization, the cooperation of a certain portion of the population who thought that Hellenization would be a good idea. You can read about that at greater length and in more detail, in 1 Maccabees, right from the beginning of that book through the end of the 4th chapter. The same thing is discussed in 2 Maccabees from chapter 3 to chapter 10.

By the year 167 B.C., the office of high priest had been seized by some of these cooperators. Pagan worship, if you can believe it, was begun and through the use of the Hellenistic gymnasia there was pressure on Jewish youth to be ashamed of such customs as their circumcision. The gymnasia, of course, like our word gymnasium, this was a program of both exercise and schooling of tremendous cultural pressure. You see a description of it in 1 Maccabees in the 1st chapter, 2 Maccabees in the 4th chapter.

In the year 169, Antiochus desecrated the Temple and confiscated the sacred vessels. That's described in 1 Maccabees :1, 2 Maccabees:5. Then with an utter disdain for what the religion of the Jewish people was, he set up an altar to the Olympian Zeus within the Temple. This is the abomination of desolation that is referred to in the book of Daniel. One sees it, for instance, in chapter 9, verse 27, one sees it in chapter 11, verse 31 and yet again, in chapter 12, verse 11. This is the abomination of desolation that just thoroughly disgusted them.

Antiochus made Jewish religious practice into a crime, a crime of treason, and he required the local authorities to accept the notion that the God of Israel was simply identical to the Greek Zeus, with Antiochus himself serving as the earthly regent in this part of the world. Some aristocrats tried to adapt themselves to Greek ways. One sees this struggle recounted again in 1 Maccabees; you see a lot of it in the first chapter, there's a description of it in the sixth chapter, and again in the eleventh chapter. On the other hand, other parts of the people, including some aristocrats, resisted, some of them violently. We hear, for instance, about the great Maccabean revolt that did eventually regain possession of the Temple and in the year 164 purified the Temple.

Still others, this is a group called the Hasidim, encouraged resistance. On the other hand, they wanted no part in violence. It seems to have been someone from this group of the Hasidim who wrote the book of Daniel in the year 165 B.C. or thereabouts. That is, after the desecration of the Temple but before the death of Antiochus. One will see more details about this within the book of Daniel in chapter 11. The passage from verse 21–45 gives some of the details of this. There is, of course, a problem about when exactly this book was edited and that's a scholarly problem we'll look at in due time. It's possible that the chapters 1–6 are actually much earlier, or maybe they come from this exact period.

Let's turn now to the historical setting of the book because the historical setting of the book is a little different than the historical setting of the composition of the book. The story that is recounted in Daniel doesn't come from the time of Antiochus when all of this confusion was going on about the abomination of desolation. That is, that's the situation that prompts its composition, but the story that's actually told comes from much earlier. It comes from that time in Israel's previous great crisis, namely, the beginning of the exile. For the northern kingdom, that exile began in the year 721 B.C., for the southern two tribes, the exile began in the year 587 B.C. and it continued for both the north and the south until the year 539 B.C. The story that is found in Daniel is about that time period.

The brilliant young man, Daniel, serves under the kings of the Babylonians and the Medes, when Israel is in its exile, just like the figure of Joseph from the book of the Genesis, served under Pharaoh. All of this is in play here. The Genesis story, chapters 37–50 tells about Joseph. One also hears, of course, about Esther with King Ahasuerus in Persia; that story is told in the first couple of chapters of Esther. Here we're focusing on the figure of Daniel who is said to live near the beginning of the exile, over there in exile serving the Persian king.

If one were expecting complete historical accuracy, that is, if this were a book about history, one would get different details but it's not so much a book about history. It's like a historical novel; it's trying to use a story with a historical setting for something that's occurring at the time of Antiochus Epiphanies. So if we were expecting complete historical accuracy, we could take issue with some of the details in Daniel. The dating for the Medes and the Persians is off. There's a problem about the identification of the figure here that's called Belshazzar who was really the son of Nabonidus, not the son of Nebuchadnezzar, and not a king. Likewise, there are problems about the dates of Darius the Mede. My point is, we need not be particularly concerned about some of those inaccuracies in the book of Daniel, about the historical dating, because it's not primarily a historical, it's a wisdom tale. In fact, except for this book of Daniel, there is no historical information about the character Daniel, unless perhaps he is the person who is mentioned in passing by the prophet Ezekiel as someone associated with Noah and Job. All of which goes to say, there isn't historical detail here. If you want, look that up; that's in Ezekiel 14:14 and 28:3.

Much more to the point, the stories from the first six chapters of the book of Daniel are edifying accounts about God's deliverance of courageous young men, Daniel and his friends, who were prepared to die for their faith. And thus, they are in a situation that is not at all unlike that situation that was faced by the youth whom the Hasidim were concerned to prepare for resistance to the pressures of King Antiochus IV Epiphanes and they wanted their young men to resist Antiochus without resorting to the violence of the Maccabees. Setting the stories of Daniel so much earlier, that is, setting these stories during the Babylonian exile at the court of Nebuchadnezzar, Belshazzar and Darius testifies to the fact that troubles of this sort had happened before; that the community could take heart from the fact that the earlier members of their community had met this and that God could be trusted to provide courage in the face of persecution. God could be trusted to provide wisdom when that wisdom was especially needed.

As a model for those who were being pressured to worship the statue of Zeus that had been set up in the Temple—for that story, see chapter 3 verses 16–18 and the related story over in the first chapter of Maccabees and the sixth chapter of 2 Maccabees—the stories about the youths who refused to worship Babylonian gods would have been specially pertinent. Hence the book of Daniel begins with that; it's chapter 1, verses 8–16. The astonishing way in which Daniel criticizes the use of the sacred vessels from the Temple in Jerusalem for a royal feast here in Babylon, that's in chapter 5, presumably applies to the robbery that Antiochus had done against the Temple that's described in 1 Maccabees. The miraculous delivery of these three young men from the fiery furnace, Daniel chapter 3, and the rescue of Daniel himself from the lion, chapter 6, almost the whole chapter, would illustrate God's readiness to protect those who are faithful to him during trials. That's the basic story.

Let's turn now and take a look at the wisdom elements that are found within the book of Daniel and see why it's so important to consider this within our course on biblical wisdom literature. We begin, there in the opening description of Daniel and his friends, to see the wisdom that God gives to his faithful ones. That opening description stresses how much they have been trained in wisdom and how much they refuse to be corrupted by some foreign wisdom; chapter 1, verses 3–8. In a way, Daniel strikes me as an example here within this story, of the ideal sage that we had seen. If you turn back to the book of Sirach, you'd find it at chapter 39, verses 1–5. There's a portrait there of what the ideal sage should be. Daniel is a living instance of it.

After a period of testing during which Daniel and his companions—interestingly they get renamed as Shadrach, Meshach, and Abednego—after a period of testing for Daniel and his friends, they receive now a diet that is limited to water and vegetables. That is, they don't want to eat any of the things from the king's table and yet as the result of this period of testing, when they ask for this very frugal diet, they turn out to be much better prepared. They found they've turned out to be much healthier and they surpass those who are eating from the king's table. It says, according to the text, they prove "ten times better" than all the magicians and enchanters at Nebuchadnezzar's court; that's in verse 20 of the first chapter.

When the sages whom Nebuchadnezzar commanded to interpret some dreams that had been troubling him, prove unable to do so, Daniel and his friends get called upon. Now, it's understandable that those sages in the court of Nebuchadnezzar couldn't interpret his dreams because interestingly, the king wouldn't even tell them what the dreams were. Presumably he didn't want to compromise the interpretation so he wanted them to tell the answer, to tell what the dreams were and what the interpretation was and they couldn't. The same charge, the same challenge is given to Daniel. Daniel directs his companions to pray. Verse 18 of chapter 2 says that he directed his friends to "seek mercy of the God of heaven concerning this mystery." He tells them to do that so that they will not perish. God then reveals the mystery to Daniel in a night vision, chapter 2 verse 19.

With utter modesty about his own powers, verse 30, Daniel testifies that it is God who reveals mysteries and that it is God who has made known the future to Nebuchadnezzar in his dream. Daniel then recounts the image from the dream even though Nebuchadnezzar hasn't told him: a figure with a golden head, with silver arms and breast, with a bronze belly and thighs, and most importantly, feet of iron and clay that are suddenly shattered by this extraordinary stone that then turns into a great mountain. It's a great vision, what a dream, chapter 2, verses 31–35.

When Daniel then interprets the image in terms of Nebuchadnezzar's golden reign as passing onto other kingdoms—a kingdom of silver, a kingdom of bronze, a kingdom divided into iron and clay—and then reference to a kingdom "that shall never be destroyed nor shall its sovereignty be left to another people"—that's verse 44— Nebuchadnezzar is astounded that Daniel knows what the dream was, let alone has an interpretation. And so Nebuchadnezzar appoints Daniel and his friends to positions of honor and rule; that's chapter 2, verse 48.

However, before long, those jealous of their positions reveal that Daniel's three companions have been refusing to worship Nebuchadnezzar's golden statue and affronted by this refusal on their part to worship them, Nebuchadnezzar has those three young friends of Daniel cast into a fire that he has heated seven times more than usual, but low and behold, when he looks in, they, plus some mysterious fourth figure, one whom chapter 3 verse 25 says is, "like a son of the gods," they are unburned. Nebuchadnezzar chalks this up to the protection that their own God has provided for them—chapter 3 verse 28—and he frees them from the fire.

There is some additional material that is found at this point in the Greek text that comes from Septuagint, that is the Jewish translation into Greek made in the 2nd century, but is not in the Hebrew or the Aramaic versions. In some Bibles, you'll find it printed in between verse 23 and verse 24 of chapter 3. In other Bibles they won't print it there but they'll put it in a footnote or they'll print it separately as part of the Apocrypha. This material is called the Song of Azariah and the Song of the Three Young Men. Very much like Psalm 148, the songs here, the Song of Azariah and the Song of the Three Young Men, illustrate the piety of the Hasidim in the way that the three young men who have been thrown into the fire place their entire confidence in God's ability to do a miracle on their behalf.

Daniel also has to interpret another dream, a dream about a very strong tree that gets stripped of its branches. This time the king does explain the details; it's chapter 4, verses 4–18. Daniel treats it as a warning about the likelihood of the king being deposed. In fact it proves true and thereby elicits on the part of some of those around, stronger faith in God; that's chapter 4, verses 19–37.

Yet another episode; while drinking out of sacred vessels from the Temple, the successor Belshazzar experiences a terrifying scene of a disembodied hand—sort of just about from here up—that writes a message on the wall that proves unintelligible to everybody except to Daniel, who can read and he reads it as, "Mene, Tekel, and Parsin." Or in some translations, "Mene, Tekel, Peres;" that's chapter 5, verse 25. Daniel explains the words as God's judgment against the sacrilege of drinking from these sacred vessels from the Temple. That very night, Belshazzar is slain and the kingdom is given to Darius the Mede; that's chapter 5, verse 30.

The final episode recounted in this portion is one in which Daniel is thrown into the lion pit for daring to pray to his God and thereby to violate the laws that he regards, as far as he knows, as "the unchangeable laws of the Medes and the Persians." His miraculous deliverance from death elicits a prayer of faith from King Darius—that's chapter 6, verse 25–27—and then he allows Daniel to prosper into the year of King Cyrus, who incidentally is the king whom God would eventually use to bring home the people, back from Babylon, back to Palestine, at the end of their exile in the year 539 B.C.

Well, looking at this whole section, what we have is a set of dreams and visions. It is not merely Freudian psychology that has seen significance in dreams. The ancient world had a profound sense of their importance. Modern psychology tends to focus on the way in which the unconscious has of playing out problems that are bothering us. Generally, it is not so much that dreams are considered a source of wisdom, but that a recurrent dream might just be tipping us off to something that's important and needs careful evaluation. The ancient world, on the other hand, had a tremendous respect for dreams. What they liked to do though, was to see the need to discern carefully. There's a wonderful description of all this in C. S. Lewis's book *The Discarded Image*. The ancient world, he tells us, had a seven-fold classification system, you see it in Cicero and Macrobius and Boethius, on all the different types of dreams and the ways in which to discern what was trustworthy and what was not.

The Bible too, has considerable respect for dream visions. In addition to the ones discussed here in Daniel, one thinks of the importance of dreams for figures like Abraham and Joseph, in the book of Genesis. What is distinctive about the biblical perspective is a willingness to hold that some dreams can come from God. While this is not at all some naïve blank check for trusting every dream, it is a claim that dreams can be a way in which God communicates wisdom to men. It is this limited sort of claim that is under discussion here. The text of Daniel turns next to Daniel's own dreams and visions, and we'll follow out that text with all of those dreams and visions in our next lecture. That lecture will also reflect on the significance of Daniel as a wisdom book.

Lecture Twenty-Seven
Daniel—God's Providential Plan for History

Scope:

The latter portions of the book of Daniel concern eschatology—that is, theological reflections on the end times. This lecture will examine chapters 7 to 12, with their mysterious references to a wisdom figure called "Son of Man," the theme of messianic hope, and the additional materials (chapters 13–14) from the Greek text. Like the book of Sirach, the book of Daniel offers an approach to the question of where to seek wisdom by looking to history and to a theology of history. This lecture will consider the book of Daniel by a consideration of its allusions and comments on the various stages of the world's history taken as parts of God's providential plan. The portions of this book about the revelation of God's eternal purpose through the angels will provide an opportunity to reflect on the nature of revelation and its relation to wisdom.

Outline

I. Wisdom themes in Daniel 7–12.

   A. The technical name for the genre that we find in the second six chapters is "apocalyptic"—a form that uses various symbols to disclose the plan of God for the world in light of a final universal judgment.

   B. In Daniel, we find the combination of prophetic urgency in summoning the people to repentance with the wisdom literature's traditional stress on the fear of the LORD as the beginning of wisdom and virtue.

   C. Just as the figure of Daniel was marked in the first section by his understanding of the plan of God within dreams, in this second section he is given the wisdom of God through an angel so as to grasp the way in which God is directing history.

II. Daniel's visions.

   A. Daniel 7:1–28. Upon inquiry (7:16), Daniel learns that this vision showed successive earthly kingdoms, the persecution of the holy ones (Hasidim), and God's own establishment of his kingdom.

B. Daniel 8:1–27. As the language of the text returns from Aramaic to Hebrew, we see a ram with two horns of unequal heights whose charges no one could withstand. The ram dominates until the coming of a goat from the west with a single horn. The goat grows magnificent, but its horn eventually breaks and gives way to four horns. From one of them came a horn that grew great and dominated the sanctuary where sacrifices are made. The period of the desolation is to last "2,300 evenings and mornings" until the sanctuary is restored.

C. Daniel 9:1–27. After Daniel recognizes that the desolations of Jerusalem must last 70 years, he confesses his own sins and the transgressions of the people to God. Gabriel then comes to Daniel during the evening sacrifice and gives a mysterious timetable ("70 weeks of years"— perhaps 70 × 7, or 490-some years) for the completion of the necessary atonement, the coming of an anointed one (*messiah*), the destruction of the holy city, and a "strong covenant."

D. Daniel 10:1–12:13. After three weeks of mourning, Daniel receives a vision about the history from Cyrus the Persian to the defeat of Antiochus. Gabriel bids Daniel not to fear and strengthens him in his weakness. Daniel is urged to persevere through troubled times.

III. Resurrection of the body in Daniel, chapter 12.

A. In the last chapter of this section there occurs, for the first time in the Bible, an explicit reference to the resurrection of the body.

B. While this theme is not developed very far here, it is of great interest for the study of biblical wisdom literature, especially in view of the problem of the righteous and just who suffer and die while the unjust and those who persecute them prosper.

C. There are also some references in the Psalms that might have bearing here.

IV. The deuterocanonical materials.

    A. The Greek version of Daniel is regarded as part of the deuterocanonical section for Catholics and Orthodox, and as part of the apocrypha for others. The Greek text for chapter 13 that is translated in most Bibles is not the Septuagint but another Greek translation, called the Theodotion translation after the name of the translator.

    B. Like the stories in the first six chapters, these stories are tales of heroic virtue. By the achievement of justice here we have not only an important wisdom theme in the tradition of Proverbs and Sirach, but a portrayal of Daniel as a young Solomon.

    C. In the final stories, we find Daniel confronting false worship. The stories are set in the time of King Cyrus of Babylon.

V. Overview.

    A. All considered, the book of Daniel is different from the main streams of biblical wisdom literature that we have seen in the didactic lessons of Proverbs and Sirach as well as from the dramatic presentations of the philosophical search for wisdom in Job and Qoheleth. Nor is it the lyrical poetry of Song of Songs.

    B. In a trajectory that runs from Sirach to the Wisdom of Solomon, there is a great concern with God's role in history. Where Sirach and Wisdom look back on the role of divine providence in giving wisdom to guide his chosen people, the visions of Daniel look ahead to the guidance God will provide.

    C. In addition, for the first time, the Bible presents a picture of resurrection from the dead, and this notion will prove to be very important for the next book that we study, the Wisdom of Solomon.

Suggested Reading:

Davies, *Daniel*.

Duggan, *The Consuming Fire*, 486–99.

Questions to Consider:

1. What is the difference between the first and second sections of this book?

2. How would you define "apocalyptic"? What are the likenesses and differences between this version of the apocalyptic genre and others that you may know (e.g., Revelation in the New Testament)?

3. What are the chief characteristics of the figure of Daniel as he appears in this book?

Lecture Twenty-Seven—Transcript
Daniel—God's Providential Plan for History

The latter portions of the book of Daniel concern eschatology, that is, the theological reflection on the end times. This lecture will examine chapters 7–12 of that book with their mysterious reference to a wisdom figure called the Son of Man and the theme of messianic hope. We'll also look at the additional materials, chapters 13 and 14, that come only in the Greek text of the book. Like the book of Sirach, the book of Daniel offers an approach to the question of where to seek wisdom by looking to history, in fact, to a theology of history. This lecture will consider the book of Daniel by a consideration of the illusions and the comments on the various stages of the world's history, all taken as part of God's providential plan. The portions of the book that are about the revelation of God's eternal purpose through the angels will provide an opportunity to reflect on the nature of revelation and its relation to wisdom and the wisdom literature tradition.

Let's turn then to chapters 7–12, that is, the second half of the book of Daniel. We'll also look eventually at those two chapters at the end that are considered part of the deuterocanonical version in chapters 13 and 14. There are any number of interesting wisdom elements in this section from Daniel 7–12. The first term we need to concern ourselves with is the word apocalyptic. This is a technical name for the genre that we find in the second six chapters. Quite distinct from Apocrypha, which is a term we've been using before to name books that are not regarded as part of the canon, this is something else. Apocalyptic is a form that uses various symbols to disclose the plan of God for the world and all of this done in light of a final universal judgment.

In the last of the prophets, from about the 4th century B.C., there is a stress on using this apocalyptic. It's presented as a final decisive battle that will take place between God and his enemies. For example, one sees this in the prophet Joel, chapters 3 and 4. One sees it in the 14th chapter of the prophecy of Zachariah. One of the major prophets, Ezekiel, has an apocalyptic in chapters 38 and 39. There's a section of Isaiah from chapter 24 to chapter 27 and that section has a very interesting part about the "day of the LORD," the day on which God will carry out his judgment. One sees this is in Amos;

one sees this in Zephaniah. In the New Testament, there's an entire book by the name of the Apocalypse.

In the book of Daniel, we find the combination of prophetic urgency in summoning the people to repentance, along with the wisdom literature's traditional stress on fear of the LORD as the beginning of wisdom, as the source of virtue. Within this portion of the book from chapter 7 to chapter 12, we will see frequent reappearance of this theme, that the wicked will fail despite their power and that those who are wise and righteous will somehow prevail. If you want to find it in the text, chapter 7 from verses 23–28 has it. Likewise chapter 11 has it starting at around verse 32 and then the first three verses of chapter 12. Not even death will conquer the wise who persevere, for chapter 12 tells us there will be a resurrection from the dead.

Just as the figure Daniel was marked in the whole first section of the book by his understanding of the plan of God within dreams, in this second section, he will be given the wisdom of God by supernatural means, namely through an angel so that he can grasp the way in which God is directing history. Take a look, if you will, at chapter 9, verse 22 and chapter 10, verse 12.

We need to look at Daniel's visions in this second half of the book. Daniel himself does not always claim to have understood these visions. Scholarship has been divided considerably on how to interpret them. While I can't possibly settle all those questions here, given the vast numbers of interpretations that a modern scholarship and ancient and medieval scholarship for that matter has offered, let me simply list the four visions and then give a pretty standard view of them.

The first one is one that comes in the seventh chapter of the book of Daniel, after the emergence from the sea of four great beasts: first there's a lion with eagle wings which is frequently a symbol for the Babylonian Empire, and a flesh-devouring bear, a four-headed winged leopard and a beast with iron teeth and ten horns, then suddenly another figure, an Ancient of Days who's presiding over a court with the books of judgment. The fourth beast is destroyed. The others are deprived of their dominion and a very interesting but mysterious figure, one that is called, according to the text, "like a son of man," is presented to the Ancient of Days and this figure is given everlasting dominion over the whole world. Upon inquiry Daniel learns, at verse 16, that the vision showed successive earthly kingdoms; the persecution of the holy ones and God's own establishment of his kingdom. The word that sometimes is translated holy ones or devout ones, is this Hasidim that I referred to when I was discussing the composition. The word *hasid*, in Hebrew, means steadfast love and it indicates a kind of a holiness because of one's charity but also by virtue of one's fidelity.

In addition to the consolation that is taken by the community of the Hasidim, from an interpretation that confirms and expands the same basic message that we saw back in the second chapter of Daniel, Christian interpreters throughout the ages have also focused on this text and they have been very ready to see the prophecy of Christ here in the figure of the Son of Man. Part of the reason is that Jesus himself uses that title of himself at any number of places in the Gospel. There's also a way in which the Christian interpreters of this particular passage, this vision, have seen it as foretelling the establishment of the kingdom of God that Jesus brought. Jesus clearly takes the term from Daniel upon himself. In the Gospel of Mark, for instance, at chapter 13, verse 26; in chapter 14 at the tail end, there at verse 62. We'll have occasion to look at some related questions in that respect in the final lectures of this course when we consider the wisdom parables of Jesus and his own proclamation of the Kingdom of God but I wanted to call attention to it here because of the use we'll make of it later.

The second one, in the book of Daniel, comes in chapter 8, verses 1–27. As the language of the text returns here from the Aramaic—that the last few chapters have been in, comes back now to Hebrew—we see a vision in which there is a ram with two horns of unequal height and the charges of this are such no one can withstand them. Daniel inquires, "What is this about?" and the angel Gabriel, appears. In fact, if we're doing the record of the Bible chronologically, this is the first appearance in the Bible of the angel Gabriel. The angel Gabriel explains that these are the kings of the Medes and the Persians that are being seen here. The ram dominates until the coming of a goat out of the west with a single horn. This is presumably the kingdom of Greece under Alexander the Great. After the victory of the ram, the goat grows magnificent but eventually its horn breaks off and where it breaks off it gives way to four horns, interpreted often as the division of Alexander's empire. From one of these comes a horn that grows very, very great and dominates the whole sanctuary where sacrifices are made. Presumably, this is a reference to what Antiochus did when he desecrated the Temple. There's an interesting reference here to the time that this all supposed to take, the period of the desolation is said to last "2,300 evenings and mornings" until the time when the sanctuary is restored; a very interesting vision.

The third vision comes in the ninth chapter of Daniel. After Daniel recognizes, from the book of Jeremiah, that the desolations of Jerusalem have to last 70 years—presumably he's making use of what we call Jeremiah 25:11, maybe Jeremiah 29:10—Daniel confesses his own sins and the transgressions of his people. He pleads with God for forgiveness for these transactions against the covenant. He embarks on a course of fasting, wearing sackcloth, sprinkling himself with ashes. In acknowledging that the calamities that the people have been suffering are due to their own sins, his prayer does not make any claim to righteousness but simply begs for God's mercy. Gabriel then comes again, comes to Daniel during the evening sacrifice; this is at chapter 9, verse 21 to give him what the following verse calls "wisdom and understanding." Gabriel then gives a mysterious timetable. It's so interesting how the chronology starts to come into some of these books and what Gabriel says is, "seventy weeks of years." Now, that could mean 70 times seven or 490 years. For the time for the completion of the necessary atonement, a long time, then there will be the coming of an anointed one, a messiah and then the destruction of the holy city, and the making of a strong covenant. One can see here what possible use Christians have made of this, for it heads toward the time about the coming of Christ, whom Christians understand as the Messiah, 70 years later in 70 A.D., the destruction of Jerusalem by the Romans and the strong covenant, a reference perhaps to the New Testament or at least sometimes Christian interpreters have so seen it.

The anointed one that's referred to here could very well be a reference to Cyrus of Persia. As I urged in the last lecture, all of this book is written in the period from the 2nd century but it refers to this period back in the 530s, back in the 540s B.C. So this is something that's already known. The anointed one, the messiah that's referred to here, could very well be Cyrus of Persia who ended the exile for the chosen people in the year 539 B.C. Another possibility is that it refers to a high priest by the name of Joshua whose story is told in the book of Ezra 3:2. Joshua presided over the rebuilding of the altar of sacrifice once the people had returned to Palestine. There was such an enormous concentration on having the temple built again, the reconsecration of the altar, so the sacrifices could begin. So it's possible that he is the messiah that is referred to here. Yet another possibility is the high priest, Onias III. Onias III was murdered while he was in exile in the year 171 B.C., and in a way, this is sometimes dated as the beginning of the persecution that Antiochus enforced. Following the almost unanimous view of the Fathers of the Church, many Christians have seen in the reference here to a messiah, a prophecy of Christ, and they liken the words about the destruction of the Temple to Jerusalem in the year 70 and there's a reference to Jesus foretelling this in the Gospels, for example at Matthew 24:15.

Let's turn now to the fourth of the visions; this is in Daniel chapter 10 through chapter 12, verse 13. After three weeks of mourning—we don't know exactly what that is, but it might refer to the interruption in the rebuilding of the Temple that occurred just then, that story is told in the fourth chapter of Ezra—but after three weeks of mourning, Daniel finally receives a vision, perhaps again in the person of Gabriel. But this time the name is not mentioned, and it's a vision this time about the history from Cyrus the Persian all the way down to the defeat of Antiochus. Now this is something the author would've known, whereas for Daniel, it's looking ahead to the future. Daniel again falls into a deep trance; this is verse 9 of chapter 10. It's like the trance when Gabriel addressed him back in the eighth chapter and in the trance, Gabriel bids Daniel, have no fear and he strengthens him where Daniel is feeling weak. Gabriel then explains the events that are to come, including symbolic references to such kings as Xerxes I, who was king from 486 B.C. to 465 B.C., references to Alexander the Great, to various of the Ptolemies and the Seleucids, all leading up to Antiochus IV Epiphanes and the great persecution. Then eventually, when you go ahead to chapter 12, verse 1, to the victory that is to be won by the angel Michael, the protecting angel of Israel. Daniel is urged by Gabriel, who's letting him see all this in Daniel's future, Daniel is urged to persevere through troubled times.

Now, the immediate message is clear; don't live for this world, live for God. That is, where Daniel is getting all of this by way of vision, there's a message intended for the reader: live for God. All these terrestrial states are only temporary staging points in light of God's ultimate authority and God's ultimate plan. One must have faith, one must have trust in God, one must obey his law regardless of the price. There's high value in being willing to sacrifice one's life for God and the text toward the end of chapter 11 from verses 33–35 brings that out nicely.

Let me turn now to the description of the next chapter because it's so significant for the themes that we've been working on throughout this course in biblical wisdom literature, namely, the theme about what happens after death, because in the twelfth chapter of Daniel, there's a description of resurrection from the dead. In the material that we get here, for the very first time in the Bible there is an explicit reference to resurrection of the body; this is chapter 12, verse 3:

> And many of those who sleep in the dust of the earth shall awake, some to everlasting life and some to shame and everlasting contempt. And those who are wise shall shine like the brightness of the firmament; and those many to righteousness, like the stars forever and ever.

These individuals here are identified as the "wise," who have been obedient to the Law. They did not yield during persecution and they will be given a fullness of life beyond death; that's the next five verses or so.

While this theme is not developed very far here, merely stated, it is of great interest for the study of biblical wisdom literature when seen as a grand trajectory, especially in view of the problem of the righteous and the just, who suffer and who die while the unjust and those who persecute them prosper. It will be taken up again in the Wisdom of Solomon, which we will begin to study in the next lecture. But first, I'd like just to dwell on this topic for a little bit by looking at some other biblical passages just to consider how the Bible treats that question of the afterlife.

There had been earlier suggestions about the possibility of a resurrection, including with the apocalyptic section from the book of Isaiah. There's a text there we should read, it's from the Isaiah 26:19: "Thy dead shall live, their bodies shall rise. O dwellers of the dust, awake and sing for joy! For the dew is a dew of light, and on the land of the shades thou wilt let it fall."

In a passage like that, there could very well be a connection to Ezekiel's symbolic vision of the return of God's people from death,

Ezekiel 37. One also sees a similar passage where there's an awakening from the dead in Isaiah 66:24.

These are very curious passages, that is, they don't get a lot of play, they don't get a lot of development elsewhere in the Old Testament. And I'm noticing them because they're there, not because they're the mainstream or because they have a long development. There are also some interesting references in the Psalms that might have a bearing on this question. For instance at Psalm 17, there's a passage that reads: "Deliver my life from the wicked with Your Sword, with your hand from men, O LORD, from men of the world who have their portion in this life."

Now that adverts to the problem but doesn't make it clear. We could be tempted to interpret this line in light of something like Jesus's parable about Lazarus and Dives in which Jesus is portraying Abraham as clearly speaking with people in the afterlife; that's in Luke 16.

Strictly speaking, however, that passage from the psalm, it doesn't say quite enough to say that we've got an unequivocal reference to life after death, likewise, Psalm 49. Interestingly, it notes that no human being can avoid death; apparently death is a permanent state. A Christian may well be inclined to see in the references to paying the price of salvation, a task that Christ alone could provide, but that could also be reading the psalm with the spiritual senses that I was discussing when we were considering the Song of the Songs. The psalm by itself doesn't yet make that clear and it seems be talking only about the inevitably of death. Let me read it and you can try to make a judgment. This is Psalm 49, beginning at verse 8.

> For the redemption of their souls is costly,
> And it shall cease forever …
> For he sees wise men die;
> Likewise the fool and the senseless person perish
> And leave their wealth to others.
> Their inner thought is that their houses will last forever,
> Their dwelling places to all generations;
> They call their lands after their own names.
> Nevertheless man, though in honor, does not remain;
> He is like the beasts that perish.
> This is the way of those who are foolish,
> And of their posterity who approve their sayings.

In a text like that, it is only the first line that gives that hint about a redemption of them, somehow a buying back, and that's what Christian often focus on. The rest of the psalm seems to talk about the fact that otherwise, one who's dead stays dead. It is part of the great mystery of trying to solve this problem. There are a considerable number of such references within the Psalms. None positively excludes the idea that God might himself rectify the situation by bringing about a resurrection of the dead, but none of them clearly affirm it. Perhaps they merely suggest a way in which life will continue by being in the memory of one's descendants, or one's life will go on by the way one lives in one's children. Now especially because I feel so strongly about the thesis that divine revelation is sequentially revealing more and more about immortality and the resurrection—things like Daniel, things like the wisdom of Solomon, and then eventually Jesus—precisely because I'm so strongly committed to that thesis, that there is a gradual disclosure of this in the history of revelation, it's important for me to look at the counterevidence, the evidence for the lack of any clear revelation on this topic from earlier in the tradition.

Let me quote some of these other passages from the Psalms that give the impression, I think, that there's nothing that comes after death so that we'll have the whole story here. For instance in Psalm 6:5: "For in death there is no remembrance of You; in the grave who will give You thanks?" That occurs in the context of a psalm which is trying to make the point, we must pray and praise God now. We must give thanks to God. We must give our thanks to God now because there is no life beyond that. Here's another text, this is from Psalm 30:9, "What prophet is there in my blood, when I go down into the pit? Will the dust praise you? Will it declare your truth?" The translation that is used in that particular passage talking about the pit is a word in Hebrew which is *Sheol* and the descriptions of *Sheol* that we get are minimal. The impression is something dungy and dark and damp and dirty. The impression is that the dead go there and that that's all there is. It's not that the wicked go there where the just go to heaven. It's not that the just go there and the wicked go to fires. The impression is this is where everybody goes. I find it very curious that through most of the Old Testament, there is no description of life in heaven. There isn't much said about it one way or the other and instead, in so far as the question comes up about the afterlife, this is about as much as one gets. There will be much more reference as we get to this later apocalyptic literature and eventually through the New Testament.

Let's continue our survey in that regard. The next passage is from Psalm 49:17–19, it reads:

> For when he dies, he shall carry nothing away; His glory shall not descend after him. Though while he lives he blesses himself (for men will praise you when you do well for yourself). He shall go down to the generation of his fathers. They shall never see light.

There's a sense of continuity from one generation to the next. There's a sense that there's somewhere we go and that is part of the perplexity, I think, when anyone is trying to read these passages. If it's not just that we cease to exist and the body corrupts, but that we go somewhere, where is this place that we go and what happens? We do not hear the answer to that.

In Psalm 88:10–12:

> Will you work wonders for the dead?
> Shall the dead arise and praise You?
> Shall Your loving kindness be declared in the grave?
> Or Your faithfulness in the place of destruction?
> Shall Your wonders be known in the dark?
> And your righteousness in the land of forgetfulness?

I love that particular passage. Not only does it talk about the *hasid* of God, that same word that is at the root of the Hasidim that we've been speaking about, but it's a series of rhetorical questions. Now the trouble with rhetorical questions is that they're just that, they're questions and we don't hear the answer. The expected answer is, no, there's nothing coming from the dead. The dead won't praise you, nothing of that will occur. On the other hand, these are intended as exhortations. Be sure to praise God now, thank God now, live according to his covenant and according to Torah, and yet they raise the question, as the opening line of the passage I just read did, when suggesting, "Shall the dead arise and praise you." And it gives that question which raises the inquiry in our minds, is there a resurrection from the dead. It's a position eventually that the Pharisees will adopt that there is a resurrection, where the Sadducees insist that there is not.

At Psalm 146, we hear the following:

> Do not put your trust in princes,
> Nor in a son of man in whom there is no help.
> His spirit departs, he returns to his earth;
> In that very day his plans perish.

Now, most directly that passage is about the fact that one must trust God and not trust any human being. Even the phrase, son of man, there, is not taken by any of the scholars that I've read to refer to the messiah, to any of the possible candidates for the messiah, but simply to the fact that no man can save us from the inevitability of death. What that raises a question is, but can God do it, and especially when Christians get into that discussion. Part of the reason why we put our hopes upon Jesus is saying that he is more than man, that he is truly God and that this will be the source of that power of resurrection.

One last passage from Psalm 89:48–49:

> Remember how short my time is;
> For what futility have you created all the children of men?
> What man can live and not see death?
> Can he deliver his life from the power of the grave?

In so doing, that particular passage, again, reminds us of the inevitably of death and nobody would say that that's not the case. But the question is, is does the power of the grave have a complete and final hold of us or is there the power of resurrection? What we see as we go later in the biblical wisdom literature is the hope precisely for that prospect.

Let's turn back then to the book of Daniel, in particular to those final chapters that are not in the Hebrew text but only in the Greek text, the part that is regarded as deuterocanonical by the Catholic and the Orthodox traditions, but for the Jewish tradition and for most of the Protestant tradition is regarded as apocrypha. The Greek text for chapter 13 that is being translated in most of the Bibles is not the Septuagint then, but rather another Greek translation. So we're not in the Jewish Greek version, but rather in a translation into Greek that's called the Theodotian translation, after the name of the translator and this gives some very interesting material.

The material that's here is like the stories in the first six chapters in that we have tales here of heroic virtue. In the first one, the virtuous Susanna trusts that God will save her from the lecherous plans of some of the wicked elders; that's chapter 13, verses 22 and 23. And following, where she's just about ready to be slain, God inspires a very young Daniel to demonstrate the mendacity of the elders who tried to seduce her by pointing out the contradiction in their stories when he examines them separately. It's just a charming story and I hope you have a chance to read it. By the achievement of justice here, we have not only an important theme in the tradition of Proverbs and Sirach, but we have a picture of Daniel as a very young Solomon, that just as he could make a decision about the two women who were competing for the one living baby, so too this young Daniel can save the maiden Susanna from these two lecherous elders.

In the final stories, we find Daniel confronting false worship. The stories are now again set in the time of King Cyrus of Babylon. By his cleverness in coating the floor of the shrine of Bel with ashes, Daniel exposes the trickery of those who claimed that this idol, this statue of a god, was consuming the food and the wine left in the shrine each evening. By some very clever cooking, Daniel causes the dragon, whom some Babylonians were worshipping, to burst open. And then by the divine command of a rather unwilling prophet, Habakkuk, Daniel gets fed, during the time of an imprisonment, along with seven ravenous lions who only keep watch with Daniel instead of devouring him, but then when the trial is over, devour the men who plotted Daniel's destruction. When the king finds that Daniel is still alive, the king throws those seven overseers into the pit. It's a very interesting story.

Let's look at the whole. All considered, the book of Daniel is different. Admittedly, quite different from the mainstreams of biblical wisdom literature that we have seen in those didactic lessons of Proverbs and Sirach, as well as from the dramatic presentations of the philosophical search for wisdom in Job and Qoheleth. Neither is it the lyrical poetry of the Song of Songs, yet it is deeply related to biblical wisdom literature, both in its presentation of a figure whose wisdom comes from God through prayer and whose judgments are marked by a wisdom that it is divine in its inspiration.

In a trajectory that runs from Sirach to the Wisdom of Solomon, there is great concern with God's role in history. Where Sirach and

Wisdom look back on the role of divine providence in giving wisdom to guide his chosen people, the visions of Daniel, they look ahead to the guidance that God will provide. If this book is to be dated as late as scholars think, then it too is employing a kind of theology or a theological reading of history, even though it is expressed in the form of wisdom prophecy. In addition, for the first time the Bible is presenting a picture of resurrection from the dead and this will prove to be a very important notion for the book we study next, the Wisdom of Solomon.

Lecture Twenty-Eight
The Wisdom of Solomon on Divine Justice

Scope:

As in the case of Qoheleth and the Song of Songs, the Wisdom of Solomon is attributed to King Solomon, the greatest sage in Israel's history, even though its actual date of composition is much later (presumably the 1st century B.C.). Written especially for Jews whose faith was shaken by the attractions of Hellenistic Alexandria— its mystery religions and its philosophical sophistication—this book consists of three clear parts: (1) the function of wisdom in instructing the faithful about the opposite destinies awaiting the virtuous and the wicked during this life and in the afterlife, (2) the discourse of King Solomon to his fellow rulers about the origin and nature of wisdom, and (3) a recitation of the role played by divine wisdom and providence in the history of the chosen people. After reviewing the historical context and the structure of the book, this lecture will consider the opening section as it reflects on the traditional concern of biblical wisdom, the choice between the ways of virtue and vice.

Outline

I. Background.

   A. Like Sirach and the final two chapters of Daniel, the book called the Wisdom of Solomon is regarded as deuterocanonical, or apocryphal. There is no doubt that it is a book composed within the Jewish community of the Diaspora in Alexandria, but the only text that we have of the book is in Greek, so it is not in the Jewish canon of holy scripture.

   B. Like Daniel before it and anticipating the New Testament that comes later, it has a clear place for the idea of resurrection of the body, and it also mentions the idea of the immortality of the soul.

II. Historical setting for the book's composition.

  A. The victory of Pompey the Great in his campaign for Roman control of the eastern Mediterranean between 67 and 63 B.C. included not only a naval struggle against the pirate fleets then menacing the Mediterranean but also land battles against Mithridates, the king of Pontus in Asia Minor, and Tigranes, the king of Armenia.

  B. In the course of his campaign, Pompey found it advantageous to enter into the internecine struggle between two Jewish brothers, Hyrcanus (with the Pharisees) and Aristobulus (with the Sadducees).

  C. After Brutus and Cassius from Pompey's party assassinated Caesar in 44 B.C., Caesar's adopted son Octavian entered into a triumvirate with Marc Antony and Lepidus. By 42 B.C., they had defeated the forces of Brutus and Cassius at Philippi.

  D. Palestine began to be dominated by the Herodian family from the time when Antipater II, as military commander, joined forces with Hyrcanus II, whom Pompey had established as the high priest.

  E. In the 1st century B.C., the Jewish community within the metropolis of Alexandria was strongly connected to Jerusalem. Earlier in our lecture series we noted that the Septuagint was produced there and that it was there that the grandson of Jesus Ben-Sirach, who wrote his text in Jerusalem, translated it into Greek.

  F. In the decade or so before the birth of Philo, an author whose name we do not know, working under the persona of Solomon, used Greek to write the book that we are about to study.

  G. As with Sirach, the intended audience for the book seems to have been the younger generation then being attracted to forsake their religion as outdated and primitive in comparison with the enchantments of Greek culture.

  H. The Wisdom of Solomon will have an entirely different attitude toward death, and its mention of the afterlife gives a wholly different vision of things. In the third part, the book also strongly rejects the alluring mystery cults in the course of a vivid and satirical attack on idolatry.

III. Structure.

    A. The dramatic setting for the book is an address by King Solomon to the other kings of the earth.

    B. The book has three parts.

IV. The opening chapter.

    A. Perhaps it was the cosmopolitan atmosphere of Alexandria and the imperial politics of the day that prompted the author of the Wisdom of Solomon to begin his book as an address to the "rulers of the earth."

    B. Before the book concludes, it will turn to the events of Exodus, which would presumably have then been unknown to any but a Jewish authorship, but the opening chapters (depending on how we interpret several crucial terms) should presumably be read to have a rather universal flavor.

    C. In Greek, the usual translation for *Adonai* is *kyrios*, whether *Adonai* is being used as a substitute for YHWH or in its own right simply as a term of respect.

    D. The term *kyrios* in Wisdom could be heard by one familiar with Hebrew as something associated with the tetragrammaton but could equally well be heard by someone familiar only with Greek as a mark of respect—presumably for "God" (*theos*, which is used in verse 3) but understood in general as divinity.

    E. Without trying to settle all of those questions, my point here is simply to maintain that one could well understand by words like these something quite specifically Jewish (e.g., "think of YHWH and observe Torah") or something far more general (e.g., "be mindful of God and seek justice").

    F. Throughout the book, there will be good reason for thinking that both of these approaches are quite legitimate, for the author appears to have in mind both the Alexandrian community of Jews in Diaspora and the cosmopolitan community of the rulers of the earth.

V. The relation of wisdom and virtue.

    A. The inward focus of the rest of these first verses (e.g., "sincerity of heart") supports a profound connection between wisdom and virtue. This same attentiveness to conscience is manifest a few verses later.

B. There is a sequence and a direction assumed here: Wisdom is a fruit that may be expected from moral virtue. Good choices must be made, and a good character established. By contrast, wisdom will flee from someone given to foolish thinking and deceitful actions.

C. As in some of the other wisdom literature that we have examined, there is a personal way of speaking about wisdom here that is connected with the moral exhortations of the books that focus on proverbial wisdom.

D. Even the use of parallel clauses echoes the style of Hebrew verse construction, while the personal reference to "the Spirit of the LORD" (capitalized here by the Revised Standard Version) both echoes back to the wisdom poems of Proverbs, Job, and Sirach as well as looks forward to what Christians will regard as the Holy Spirit.

VI. In the next lecture we will consider the book's concern, even from its opening chapter, with life and death. What we have seen already is the pairing of the ways of virtue and vice that is highly traditional in sapiential literature.

Suggested Reading:

Clifford, *The Wisdom Literature*, chap. 7.

Murphy, *The Tree of Life*, chap. 6.

Winston, *The Anchor Bible: The Wisdom of Solomon*.

Questions to Consider:

1. How would you define "justice" and "righteousness"? These are multidimensional realities. What should we include in our ideas of justice and righteousness in order to make them full and adequate descriptions?

2. The book makes an interesting assertion about what it takes to receive wisdom when it asserts that one needs a peaceful conscience. What is conscience, and why does a guilty conscience make it hard to get an accurate perspective on things?

3. What does "the Spirit of the LORD" mean? How do you understand the references to spirit in the opening chapter of Wisdom?

The Wisdom of Solomon on Divine Justice

We turn now to the book called the Wisdom of Solomon. As in the case of Qoheleth and the Song of Songs, this book is attributed to King Solomon, the greatest sage in Israel's history, even though its actual date of composition is much later than that, probably 800 or 900 years later, because this book seems to come from the 1st century B.C. Written especially for Jews whose faith was shaken by the attractions of Hellenistic Alexandria—its mystery religions and its philosophical sophistication—this book consists of three parts. First, we have the figure of King Solomon addressing the kings of the earth and speaking especially about the function of wisdom in instructing the faithful about the opposite destinies awaiting the virtuous and the wicked during this life and in the afterlife. Then, that figure of King Solomon appears again and gives a discourse to his fellow rulers about the origin and nature of wisdom. Third, we have King Solomon's recitation of the role played by divine wisdom and providence in the history of the chosen people. After reviewing the historical context and the structure of this book, this lecture will consider the opening section as it reflects on the traditional concerns of biblical wisdom, the choice between the ways of virtue and the ways of vice.

Let's begin with some considerations about the background. Like Sirach and those final two chapters of Daniel, the book called the Wisdom of Solomon, depending on your perspective, is regarded as either deuterocanonical or apocryphal. There is no doubt that it is a book composed within the Jewish community of the diaspora in Alexandria, but the only text we have of this book is in Greek, and thus, this book does not occur in the Jewish canon of holy scripture. It is in the biblical canon accepted by the Orthodox Church and by the Catholic Church as deuterocanonical and it tends to be found in the section of Apocrypha in most Protestant communities.

Like Daniel before it and anticipating the New Testament that comes a bit later, it has a clear place for the idea of the resurrection of the body. In fact, we'll see that very near the start of the text. It also mentions the idea of the immortality of the soul. Like Qoheleth and Song of Songs, this book is ascribed to Solomon but there is very little doubt among scholars that it was composed long after the period of the actual King Solomon. In both its title and its content, it stands squarely within the tradition of biblical wisdom literature.

Let's take a look now at the historical setting of the book's composition. The victory of Pompey the Great, who lived from 106–48 B.C., his victory and his campaign for Roman control of the eastern Mediterranean between 67 and 63 B.C., included not only a naval struggle against the pirate fleets that were then menacing the Mediterranean, but also land battles against figures like Mithridates, the king of Pontus in Asia Minor, and Tigranes, the king of Armenia. In the course of Pompey's campaign, he found it advantageous to enter into the internecine struggle between two Jewish brothers, on the one hand, Hyrcanus with the Pharisees, and Aristobulus, with the Sadducees. After besieging Jerusalem, he killed more than a 1,000 Jews right in the vicinity of the Temple, and then desecrated the Temple by entering into the Holy of Holies to resolve his curiosities about the nature of Jewish worship. He showed no respect whatsoever. Later, in Rome, he was at first allied to Julius Caesar as part of the First Triumvirate, but then became Caesar's rival after the death of the third member of that triumvirate, Crassus. He was eventually assassinated in Egypt after losing the battle of Pharsalus to Caesar in 48 B.C. All of this is recounted in great detail in the book of Flavius Josephus, *The Wars of the Jews*, very near the beginning of book one.

After Brutus and Cassius from Pompey's party assassinated Caesar in 44 B.C., Caesar's adopted son, Octavian, entered into a new triumvirate with Marc Antony and Lepidus. By 42 B.C., he had defeated the forces of Brutus and Cassius at Philippi. Antony's affair and his alliance with Cleopatra of Egypt eventually led Octavian to attack Antony and eventually he defeated him at Actium in 31 B.C. Antony and Cleopatra committed suicide, and in 30 B.C., Octavian killed her son Caesarion to ensure that he alone could claim to be Caesar's legitimate heir. In 27 B.C., the Roman Senate decreed him Augustus and he reigned as Emperor of Rome until 14 A.D.

At this time, Palestine began to be dominated by the Herodian family, from the time when Antipater II as military commander joined forces with Hyrcanus II, whom Pompey had established as the high priest. Antipater's son, Herod, became governor of Galilee and cultivated the favor of a series of Roman rulers from Caesar through Cassius and Marc Antony to Octavian. The senate named him King of the Jews, in 40 B.C. on the recommendation of both Antony and Octavian, as they were sparring. He reigned there ruthlessly from 37 B.C.–4 A.D., eliminating rivals by murder and resisting Cleopatra, who wanted to extend her rule to include Judea. It was under his direction that the project of reconstructing the Temple began, as well as the construction of fortresses at Herodium and Masada, and his descendants continued to rule the area during the time of Jesus.

In the 1st century B.C., the Jewish community within the metropolis of Alexandria was strongly connected to Jerusalem; a lot of conversation, a lot of communication. Earlier in our lecture series, we noticed that the Septuagint was produced there—2nd century B.C.—and it was there that the grandson of Jesus Ben-Sirach, who wrote his text in Jerusalem, translated his grandfather's text into Greek. In the lecture that we gave on the Song of Songs, we had occasion to note the importance of the allegorical interpretation developed by the Jewish community and especially by the Jewish scholar, Philo of Alexandria, who lived from 20 B.C.–50 A.D.

In the decade or so before the birth of Philo, an author whose name we do not know used Greek to write the book that we are about to study and he did so under the persona of Solomon; so he writes it as if he's King Solomon. The content of this book and its recurrent references to the scriptures make it absolutely clear that the author is Jewish, but we can also detect a very strong acquaintance with the traditions of Hellenistic wisdom. He knows them very well, and in particular he's acquainted with Platonic and Stoic philosophy and with the science of the day.

Like Sirach, the intended audience for this book seems to have been the younger generation, then being attracted to forsake their own religion as something outdated and primitive in comparison with the novelties and the sophistications and the enchantments of Greek culture. The author is eager to show the superior wisdom of divine revelation. He does so both by attacking the foolishness of Epicurean thought and by showing how the scriptures already include most of the important lessons that Greek philosophy, especially Platonic philosophy, had to teach. That term Epicurean philosophy means the philosophy associated with the Greek thinker, Epicurus. It's a philosophy that takes the goal of life to be pleasure. Now, there are crass forms of this that are purely hedonistic. Epicurus's own views were sophisticated. He paid much attention to the different forms that pleasure could take, the different forms of pain. He had a strong sense of the ways in which certain forms of pain can be the means to longer-range pleasures. He had a sense of the different intensities of pleasures and the different durations, the quality of pleasures, in fact a whole hierarchy of them. Epicurus and then his Roman follower, Lucretius, had a strong sense that there was no God and they ridiculed belief in God. They ridiculed religious belief altogether as superstitious, something made up by those who are afraid of death. For the Epicureans, death means the utter cessation of being, life consciousness, and so they propose once you realize that death is the absolute end, there's nothing to fear. For there will be no center of consciousness to experience any pain. That'll be very significant for what we see in this book.

The Wisdom of Solomon will have an entirely different attitude toward death and its mention of the afterlife, even, near the beginning of the book, gives a wholly different vision of things. This book also strongly rejects the alluring mystery cults in the course of a very vivid and satirical attack on idolatry in the third part of the Wisdom of Solomon. In the background here, in addition to that Greek philosophy, is the curious phenomenon, always and everywhere in history I suppose, that people do need to believe in something. When philosophical rationalism—such as we found it there in Alexandria in the Hellenistic period—when philosophical rationalism had cast into doubt among the Jews there of Alexandria the truth of revealed religion, even sophisticated people still felt the need for spirituality; something to do even though they no longer believed in the religious claims.

When they fall away from belief in the God of revelation and the disciplines of Torah and the disciplines of the wisdom tradition, those who felt the need for spirituality, well some of them fell into some of the strangest sort of beliefs, just as we see happening nowadays sometimes among even sophisticated people who get into new age spirituality. In Alexandria in Egypt it was a matter of astrology. There were fertility rights. There were the bizarre rituals of the mystery religions that prospered there in Alexandria and eventually got all over the Roman Empire. This is part of the background of the book of Wisdom of Solomon, as it was to a certain degree for the book of Sirach and for the book of Daniel; a culture war, a desire to preserve religion when under the sophisticated attack of a very clever alien culture.

Let's look now at the structure of the book so as to understand better for the sake of our reading. The dramatic setting for this book is an address, an address by King Solomon to his fellow kings of the earth. It's not clear where it's taking place or what kind of an assembly at which they all would've been present, but for the sake of the book, we have King Solomon talking to his fellow kings. This interesting choice of literary framework makes it possible to show the greatest of Judaism's wisdom figures, namely Solomon, as an authority who can illuminate the rulers elsewhere from the earth. He can illuminate the wise of every land and of every faith, but in the course of this address, the author has the opportunity also to rein in some of the members of his own community who are very tempted to abandon their own faith and to embrace the enticing culture of Hellenistic Alexandria. Just imagine being confronted by the emperor of the world or by being confronted by these very important Roman generals who were fighting for the control of the Mediterranean. And that sense of, King Solomon is greater than any of these magnificent powers of his own day, I think, is in the background here of that opening.

The book has three parts. After some remarks that make it clear that the narrator is King Solomon, who is speaking to his fellow kings of the earth, what we get is a vision of righteous Jews who died for fidelity to Torah. And then quite unexpectedly, who awaken from death and suddenly those who were persecuted, now become the judges of those who had persecuted them. That's from chapter 1, verse 1 up through chapter 5, verse 23.

Then, second part, once again in the voice of King Solomon, we have an instruction given to his fellow kings on the right way to pursue wisdom. The way that Solomon himself in his own wisdom from the beginning of his life had to pursue, and he addresses this to his fellow kings. We saw before in Proverbs and in Job and in Sirach, a wisdom poem. No surprise, there is a wisdom poem here. This is part of the way in which to see the continuity between this book, even though it occurs only in Greek, and those earlier parts of the wisdom literature that belong to the revelation and the scriptures of Israel; from chapter 6, verse 1 through chapter 9, verse 18.

Finally, the third part features King Solomon offering a recital of Israel's history to illustrate the ways in which God's providential wisdom has taken such good care of his chosen people. This third part goes from chapter 10, right at the beginning, through the end of the book, chapter 19, verse 22. This section includes—besides the recounting of the story of Moses and the plagues, which is told at great length—it includes a repudiation of those nature religions and those mystery religions and it has a biting satire on idolatry of any sort; that's from chapter 13 through chapter 15, verse 19. It also has some further comments on that question of immortality of the soul and the incorruptibility of the resurrected body.

We've considered the structure, now let's turn back to the very beginning and begin our survey of the text by looking at the opening chapter: a summons to justice and righteousness. Perhaps it was the cosmopolitan atmosphere of Alexandria and the imperial politics of the day that were imperiling the Jewish people that prompted this unknown author of the Wisdom of Solomon to begin his book as an address to the "rulers of the earth," verse 1 of chapter 1, and then later to continue that same literary device in the central section of the book, chapter 6 through chapter 9.

Before the book concludes, we will turn to subjects that would presumably have then been unknown to any but a Jewish authorship. The recounting of the events of the exodus would've been part of Jewish history but not known to Romans particularly, but the opening chapter, depending on how we interpret several crucial terms, should presumably be read to have a rather universal flavor like the universalism of the Hellenistic culture of Alexandria. Well, so too the author wants to have that same universal note, I think, to attract some of those whom he hopes his book will influence.

Let's turn then to the text here. This is the first two verses of the first chapter:

> Love righteousness, you rulers of the earth,
> think of the LORD with uprightness,
> and seek him with sincerity of heart;
> because he is found by those who do not put him to the test,
> and manifests himself to those who do not distrust him.

One sees in a line like that, first, that it is the figure of Solomon talking to his fellow kings of the earth. He's quite mindful of the nature of his audience and so he's directly addressing them. Now, even if the author is intending to influence the young, the impression that they're being given is, here's their greatest ruler, King Solomon, who can sit in parley and in conference with other rulers who seem to be so powerful in his own day and you can imagine them as all ears, eager to listen in on that high-level conversation. There's also, in the part that I just read, a reference to terms like righteousness and justice. These are crucial terms. There's also the term LORD and we need to have a consideration about the meaning of those terms, especially because a term like righteousness, which will be translating a Greek term like *dikaiosune*, which means justice, has a tremendous resonance within Greek thought quite independently of the resonance that it has within Jewish thought. So we'll need to consider all of those possibilities.

There's also the term, LORD. Earlier in this course, we noted the frequent practice when the tetragrammaton YHWH appeared in a text. Because this is the sacred name of God, the practice was to substitute the word Adonai instead when it was being read. That term Adonai means, in most English translations, will be translated as "the LORD." Since this is the very name of the God given to Moses on Mt. Sinai, it may not be pronounced except on the day of Yom Kippur once a year by the high priest in the Temple. The substitute word that is pronounced in its stead, Adonai, usually is rendered in English as the LORD, and we saw it as written in small caps. But we're dealing here not just with a Hebrew text, but with a Greek text. Adonai is also a general term for someone of superior rank just as the term in English, LORD, is. It comes of course from the references of the aristocracy. One can see that, for instance, even in the text of the Hebrew scriptures at Psalm 110 where it says, "The LORD said to my LORD …" Well, the first time the LORD appears, the word Adonai is referring to the tetragrammaton, whereas the second time it's referring not to God but referring presumably to David and in that case, the word Adonai is still used but now it clearly has an earthly reference.

When we get to Greek, the usual translation for Adonai into Greek is *kyrios*. Some Christians may recognize this in the phrase *kyrie eleison*, the LORD have mercy. Whether Adonai is being used as a substitute for YHWH or whether Adonai is being used in its own right, simply as a term of human respect, both of those get translated into Greek as *kyrios* or LORD. One sees this, for instance, in the New Testament again and again, when Mary Magdalene, after the resurrection of Jesus, is addressing someone whom she thinks is the gardener in the Gospel of John 20:15. So she's not recognizing this as Jesus. She's not making any assertions about the tetragrammaton, instead she addresses him in the vocative case of the term *kyrios*. She says, *Kyrie*, my LORD, and it's just trying to be respectful, like saying sir.

My point here is that the term *kyrios* in the book of Wisdom, could be heard, presumably would be heard, by someone familiar with Hebrew as something associated with the tetragrammaton. But someone who is not acquainted with the Hebrew tradition was only associating themselves with the Greek tradition; they could well hear this simply as a general term of reverence, a general term of respect. It could include God, like the word *theos* which is used in verse 3, which in general refers to divinity of any sort but not necessarily to the God of the Hebrews. It could also, of course, refer very fully to the God that is the object of disclosure and the revelation made to the Jews.

Likewise, the term translated as righteousness in the lines I just read, *dikaiosune* in Greek, easily has as its general meaning in Greek, the term justice. Justice is defined, for instance, by an Aristotle or a Plato, it means giving to another what is fair or what is due. But the term *dikaiosune*, for someone who is mindful of the Jewish origins here, presumably that term, *diakaiosune* or justice, would also let the person hear the Hebrew word, *zedekah*, which means justice or righteousness, specifically the righteousness that comes by keeping the law. These terms then are related but distinct and in other contexts one could raise such questions as whether it is a matter of doing certain actions that are required, or perhaps having a certain virtuous disposition. But especially in light of the importance of covenant and the importance of Torah, what that *dikaiosune* or *zedekah* presumably mean is, being in right relationship to God, God being the one who makes us just.

Well, without trying to settle all of those questions, I did want to raise the point of terminology here in order to maintain, very clearly, that one can understand by words like these, something specifically Jewish, "think of YHWH and observe Torah," or something far more general, "be mindful of God and seek justice," which any Greek could accept. Throughout the book there will be good reason for thinking that both of these approaches are quite legitimate. For the author appears to have in mind both the Alexandrian community of Jews in Diaspora, but also the cosmopolitan community of rulers of the earth and the cosmopolitan Hellenistic community of Alexandria, a very vigorous city.

Let's turn now to the question of the relation, as this book sees it, the relation between wisdom and virtue. The inward focus of the rest of these initial verses, for instance there's a reference to sincerity of heart in what's coming, the inward focus of the rest of these verses supports a very profound connection between wisdom, as we've been studying it, and virtue. We saw that so often in Sirach. This is in the same tradition. This same attentiveness to good conscience, to a well-formed conscience, one that has been crafted according to the lines of Torah and of covenant, becomes very, very clear as we move forward. Let's look at the text, for instance, in chapter 1, verse 6: "For wisdom is a kindly spirit and will not free a blasphemer from the guilt of his words; because God is witness of his inmost feelings, and a true observer of his heart, and a hearer of his tongue."

Now, inwards like that, what I'm hearing is an author who is trying to show God as being alert to all that's going on inside us. If one doesn't have that sense of conscience then what one has to look to is external action. Am I keeping the commandment by what I do? That's important, but here it's also that God knows the spirit with which we do it, that God has a sense, a complete knowledge of our inner workings. And hence the notion, the strong importance, on having a well-formed conscience and a conscience that now can be peaceful for having had the right idea and the right motive or at least having corrected wayward ones.

The author tells us that divine wisdom will not be given broad spread. It will not be given to those who distrust God, rather, it will be given to those who do trust. At verse 3 for instance, it says "perverse thoughts separate men from God" or verse 4, "wisdom will not enter a deceitful soul" nor "dwell in a body enslaved to sin." There's just a strong sense here of where one can expect wisdom to flourish, where one can expect to hear God and it's that deep sense in conscience that if one's conscience is not right, one won't be able to be wise in one's decision, one will be preoccupied. Just to take a small example from our own experience. Just imagine the last time you told a lie. Perhaps you never have and that's good, but if you know of a case, the last time you shaved the truth a little bit, where there's a way in which one is so preoccupied with that, that one can't even make the right or a wise decision on the next matter because one is so very concerned with holding onto whatever lie one told so that it not be found out. I think that's the sense of this good clean conscience where wisdom can flourish.

There's a sequence then and a direction assumed here. Wisdom is a fruit that may be expected to come from moral virtue. Good choices must be made. A good character must be established. By contrast, wisdom will flee from someone given to foolish thinking, given to deceitful actions. I think that we are being given here an impression like the impression that was found so often in the pages of Proverbs and in the pages of Sirach. The busy workings of a wicked mind leave no room for peace; the good order of a mind that it is found in one who's at least trying to be righteous, allows for the contemplation of higher things, including a sense of God's plan for the world and other aspects of genuine wisdom. Let's continue to read. This is at chapter 1, verse 5:

> For a holy and disciplined spirit will flee from deceit,
> and rise and depart from foolish thoughts
> and will be ashamed at the approach of unrighteousness.

As in some of the other wisdom literature that we have examined, there is a very personal way of speaking here about wisdom that is connected with moral exhortation, much as in those books of the Proverbs and of Sirach, that personal sense of ,we must find the right course of action, we must be very attentive to the wisdom that God is giving and leading us in our choices. At verses 7 and 8 and then verse 11 within chapter 1, it reads:

> Because the Spirit of the LORD has filled the world,
> and that which holds all things together knows what it said;
> therefore no one who utters unrighteous things will
>   escape notice,
> and justice, when it punishes, will not pass him by …
> Beware then of useless murmuring,
> and keep your tongue from slander,
> because no secret word is without result,
> and a lying mouth destroys the soul.

A very strong claim there, of course. It adverts to the problem that we have been discussing since we began our course on the book of Proverbs, the opening segment of biblical wisdom literature. Namely, the expectation that there will be retribution for the wicked, that there will be a justification and a providing of a suitable reward or a vindication for the innocent. Here too, this is taken in as strong a way as we have seen it anywhere in our course. I think that part of the reason why it can be said as strongly on that, is that part of the revelation that this book claims to disclose is a revelation that even when that retribution, even when that justice, does not happen in life, it will happen after life, in the next life. And when we turn to chapter 2 we will see precisely that story about the resurrection of the dead.

Here in the text I just read, even the use of parallel clauses echoes the very traditional style of Hebrew verse construction, while the personal reference to the Spirit of the LORD—if you're following with me in the Revised Standard Version, those terms are capitalized, Spirit and LORD, and it echoes back to the wisdom poems of Proverbs and Job and Sirach, that personified figure—as well as looks forward, for Christians, looks forward to what is known as the Holy Spirit.

In the next lecture, then, we will consider this book's chief concerns, even from the opening chapter, a concern with life and death, a concern with resurrection beyond death. What we have seen already is the pairing of the ways of virtue and vice that is so traditional within sapiential literature.

Lecture Twenty-Nine
The Wisdom of Solomon on Death

Scope:

In the first five chapters of the book of Wisdom, we find important material on the traditional wisdom problem of the suffering of the innocent, in this case the tragic death of those who died for their virtuous observance of the Torah. Earlier books in the sapiential tradition had raised questions in the spirit of theodicy about God's justice and about making sense of life and history. This book finds the answer to those questions in God's gift of immortality to the virtuous and the expectation of retribution for the wicked in the afterlife. This lecture will consider the book's treatment of the topics of the covenant and the immortality of the soul.

Outline

I.   The connection between righteousness and immortality.

    A. The book opens with a set of contrasting associations between wisdom and virtue on the one hand and foolishness and vice on the other. This approach is very traditional for wisdom books.

    B. The author's first mention of death alludes to Genesis and directs us to remember the purpose of God's plan in creation.

    C. As we go forward, we will have reason to hold that it is not only physical death (death of the body) that is under discussion here, but spiritual death (death of the soul through godlessness and sin) that is the author's concern.

II. The coming of death into the world.

    A. Death is, in Genesis, the punishment of sin—we might think of it as a kind of frustration of the divine plan that God allows to happen so that human beings can exercise their freedom, for one of the requirements of freedom is that actions have their consequences.

    B. The text explicitly associated righteousness with immortality. Mainstream tradition holds that one must truly cooperate with God's grace and that without God's grace, no amount of human effort will achieve the task.

III. Persecuted and persecutors will unexpectedly change places (1:16–5:23).

    A. The rulers of the earth are addressed at the beginning of the book with the encouragement to love righteousness so that wisdom may settle upon them.

    B. No details are provided about any specific situation at the opening of the story; there is simply the case of ungodly men who have made some kind of arrangement with death.

    C. The second chapter exhibits the thought processes of these evildoers and shows that their psychology involves the denial of any existence beyond the grave and hence the lack of any reason not to try and get away with what they can during life.

    D. We might have thought such materialism a modern invention, but in antiquity this is, in substance, the position of Epicurean philosophy, and we would do well to pause for a moment on this.

    E. At the core of the Epicurean position is precisely the sort of godlessness that the Wisdom of Solomon is addressing. It was Epicurus's view that to be rid of the pain of unnecessary fear, one needs to rid oneself of the illusions of God and of the afterlife.

    F. In setting forth the reasoning here, the text portrays someone who still thinks in such biblical categories as "creation," "righteousness," and "sin" even while taking a position diametrically opposed to the Bible.

    G. Blinded by their wickedness, the speakers devise a plot to see if the righteous will hold fast to the end in their righteousness (2:13–20). The narrator, however, comments on what they failed to understand, especially what the immortal God intended when creating humankind.

IV. The suffering and death of the righteous (3:1–4:19).

    A. Chapter 3 and most of chapter 4 offer a wisdom perspective on the problem of innocent suffering by treating them from the divine perspective.

B. Like Sirach, the Wisdom of Solomon can envision that suffering can be a way to test and to purify. Some Christians subsequently applied lines like these to the doctrine of purgatory, but they also make sense when applied to earthly trials.

C. Throughout this material, the author keeps the focus on moral psychology—that is, the explanation of how it is that we deliberate about moral questions and how we come to the decisions we do.

V. The judgment of the righteous on the godless, and God's justice (4:20–5:23).

A. The dramatic surprise in the story comes with a scene that is set after the death of both parties. Suddenly, the roles are reversed, and those who were the persecuted now become the judges of their persecutors.

B. The narrator explains the result—not in some Greek philosophical argumentation like Plato's about a natural immortality but in his own distinctive approach to immortality as the gift that God gives to those who observe his commandments and honor his will.

C. I stress the difference between the approach to the question of immortality in Greek philosophy and the approach taken here, simply because some readers have interpreted this book as if it were not sufficiently biblical or were too much indebted to Greek philosophy.

D. In my judgment, it does take up some of the concerns of Greek philosophy as well as some of the vocabulary, but as our further study will continue to show, it clearly adapts the meaning of the terms borrowed from Hellenistic philosophy for its own purposes—guided, I think, by the inspiration of the God who is making this revelation.

VI. In the next lecture we will turn to the considerations that the author in the persona of Solomon addresses to the kings of the earth as a reflection on this story.

Suggested Reading:

Becker, *The Denial of Death.*

Kolarcik, *The Ambiguity of Death.*

Nickelsburg, *Resurrection, Immortality, and Eternal Life.*

Questions to Consider:

1. What does the Wisdom of Solomon hold to be at the root of all sin? How do you see it?

2. Why do people fear death (whether they think that there is an afterlife or not)? Does it make any sense to fear death if death is simply annihilation (for then presumably one will not be present to experience that annihilation)?

3. Is there a reason for persevering in moral goodness at all costs if there is nothing beyond this life?

Lecture Twenty-Nine—Transcript
The Wisdom of Solomon on Death

This lecture continues our consideration of the book called the Wisdom of Solomon. In the first five chapters of the book of Wisdom, we find very important material—especially given the long history of this subject in the wisdom literature tradition—we find very important material on that classic wisdom problem of the suffering of the innocent. In this case, the particular innocent individuals that are concerned, are those who have died for their virtuous observance of Torah. So it's not just somebody who is generally innocent but someone who's truly virtuous. Earlier books in the sapiential tradition had raised questions in a philosophical way, in that spirit of theodicy, asking about God's justice and about whether we can make sense of life and whether the patterns of history make any sense. This book finds the answer to those questions in a different place than we found it in the earlier books, namely in God's gift of immortality to those people who are virtuous. And also, it includes an expectation of retribution for the wicked in the afterlife and even the just will somehow have a role in that retribution. Hence this lecture will consider the book's treatment of various topics that are important here, the topic of covenant, the topic of justice, and the topic of the immortality of the soul.

Let's begin by considering the connection between righteousness and immortality. We've often seen some kind of connection between justice and retribution, but here it's specifically in terms of immortality. The book begins those opening lines—I'll quote in a minute from chapter 1, verses 12–15—it begins with a reflection on the fact that God did not make death. It opens with the usual pattern of contrasting associations that we've seen in other books of wisdom literature. On the one hand, wisdom and virtue, a sense that one has to really know, that's the wisdom part, and then one has to be ready to act, that's the virtue part. On the other hand, a connection between foolishness and vice. The foolishness, of course, being an inability really to receive and accept wisdom, and vice, the practice of something that's some form of wickedness or other. This approach of balancing, or maybe I should say juxtaposing, those pairs is typical of the wisdom books. And the author of this book, the Wisdom of Solomon, turns not just to the contrast but to the consequences that may be expected, and not just consequences in this life but now taking it to a new level of meaning, to life after death.

The author's very first mention of death alludes to the book of Genesis with which the Bible begins and it directs us to remember, to think very carefully, about the purpose that God had in planning creation. Let me read chapter 1, verses 12–15 for that particular passage:,

> Do not invite death by the error of your life,
> nor bring on destruction by the works of your hands;
> because God did not make death,
> and he does not delight in the death of the living.
> For he created all things that they might exist,
> and the generative forces of the world are wholesome,
> and there is no destructive poison in them;
> and the dominion of Hades is not on earth.
> For righteousness is immortal.

In a passage like that, what we're hearing, I think, are memories within Israel, memories of the catalog of all the things that God created according to the book of Genesis. There we heard it in the story of the six days and the various things that God made but also in the pattern of what God created on each day. At the end of the each day, Genesis always takes note of the fact that God saw that what he had made was good and he delighted in what he had made. That's echoed in this passage. The passage, however, makes clear and brings us to the nub of the controversy that God did not make death and that God takes no delight in it.

Part of what we as philosophers hear, I think, in a passage like that is that God made all the things that there are, but death isn't a thing. Death is rather a state when some thing ceases to exist. As we go forward, we will have reason to hold, reading this book and its comments on death, we will have reason to understand, that the author is referring not only to physical death, the death of the body that comes as the result of sin and then the interplay of natural forces, but also, a very special form of the understanding of death. Namely, spiritual death, the death that the soul undergoes when it becomes godless, when it becomes sinful and refuses to repent, refuses to change its ways. There's a kind of a spiritual death, and that both of these things are the source of concern for our author.

The author then goes on into a discussion about how death comes into the world. That is, if God made everything and God did not make death, well, how did death get there? Genesis, you will remember, Genesis regards death as a punishment for sin. That is, after Adam and Eve have sinned, God is going to give this as part of the punishment, that we'll someday have to die. We might think of it, in a way, as a kind of frustration of the divine plan that God allows to happen. Even though God is omnipotent, even though God is almighty, precisely because God gives human beings freedom, human beings can exercise that freedom. And one of the ways in which they can exercise that freedom is to frustrate the divine plan that they use their freedom well and enjoy the happiness that God intends for them. Instead, if they choose to sin, if they choose to abide in their wickedness, God will allow that, and well, in a way, he'll allow his plan to be frustrated because as we saw when we were discussing C. S. Lewis earlier on in the course, one of the requirements for beings to be free is that actions will have their consequences; that there's a stable enough natural world, that actions will have their consequences even if those actions are against the divine will and contrary to the divine plan.

The text explicitly associates righteousness with immortality. That is, it addresses head on this question about what happens to the good and the innocent who seem to be afflicted in this life. How come it doesn't all work out? This text explicitly associates righteousness with immortality, with a time and a place and a state where the just will be given their due rewards. Countless theologians have wrestled with the related problem, namely the problem of whether one can achieve righteousness on one's own; whether one's own actions can do it; whether one's own efforts can achieve it. The mainstream tradition in theology wants to hold that we cannot do so. We're expected to be good. We're expected to follow God's law. We're expected to be righteous but we can't achieve that righteousness, because of the darkness of our minds, because of the weakness of our will, sometimes because of the disordered and perverse nature of our desires. Even if we try our best, we can't achieve full righteousness and so the mainstream theological tradition thinking about this wants to say, we desperately need God's grace and we need to cooperate with that grace; that without God's grace and without our cooperation with it, no amount of pure human effort will achieve the task.

One sees some of this discussion in other books of biblical wisdom literature. One could look, for instance, to the writings of St. Paul for this. When Paul was still Saul, still a Pharisee, and very, very intent upon trying to fulfill the law, trying to achieve the righteousness that the law demands, he was concerned about this. A cornerstone of his thinking was his conviction that the quest for righteousness is something that one could achieve by keeping the law to its finest detail. This is what his school of the Pharisees practiced and what he himself tried to practice as he calls himself, a Pharisee of Pharisees. By contrast, after his conversion to Christianity, one of the keystones of his new doctrine, one of the keystones of his thinking once he's converted, is the impossibility of our ever keeping the law merely on our own, but only the possibility of keeping it when we have God's grace at hand and when we're responsive in the right way. That's getting ahead of our story though a little bit.

Right here, we're simply focusing in on the text of the book of Wisdom and the text here raises the question without settling it. It merely says in the end of the passage that I just read, "For righteousness is immortal." The text here, however, does not explain yet how we get that righteousness. It leaves some room that will be worked out in later revelation and then in the process of theological reflection on that revelation.

Let's push on though to the next part of the text, chapter 1, verse 16 all the way up to chapter 5, verse 23. This is a story, a very continuous story about some Jews who have been persecuted and their persecutors. It's not just the story of the earthly life in which this occurs, but also it's a story about what happens after death when they change places.

The very first part of it, from chapter 1, verse 16 to chapter 2, verse 24, is a description simply that sets the stage by bringing out the conflict, namely a way in which the author of the Wisdom of Solomon works on the theme that godlessness brings death. It's set by the figure of King Solomon and King Solomon is addressing the rulers of the earth. He's giving them a kind of encouragement; love righteousness, love justice, and if you will sufficiently love justice and righteousness, wisdom will come and settle upon you. The rulers to whom he is speaking are then given a story by Solomon, a story on which they are to meditate, the story of what happened to some individuals who did indeed act unjustly and to others who were treated unjustly by them. That story, beginning here at the end of chapter 1, will go all the way to the end of chapter 5. At the beginning of chapter 6, when we turn to the second part of this, it's a sort of a whole new situation, a new scene in the course of this particular play.

No details are provided here at the beginning of chapter 1 about whatever the specific situation at the opening of the story was. I can well imagine that this was something involving that situation at Alexandria where good Jews were there trying to keep Torah but were experiencing some of that conflict and challenge with Hellenism that we were discussing when we looked at, for instance, the book of Sirach. In any case, what we've got here is simply the case of really virtuous people trying to keep Torah and on the other hand, some ungodly men who have been willing to persecute them and thereby, made a kind of arrangement, a kind of covenant with death. In fact, the text here—remember it's a Greek text as we were saying in the last lecture—the Greek text uses a word, *syntheke*, that could very well be translated as contract, but I would presume that it's not just any ordinary contract. In fact it's a Greek translation with a deep biblical resonance, for this is in the Septuagint, the usual translation of the Hebrew term *berith*, that is the term for covenant.

The second chapter in the book of the Wisdom of Solomon then goes on to exhibit the thought processes of these evildoers. In a way, it's a reflection on psychology, and I think that you will find throughout the book, the Wisdom of Solomon, that there's a lot of psychological insight. We'll see this again and again as we go through the book. Here in the second chapter, what the psychological insight is, is that it shows that there's a connection between denying the existence of any life beyond the grave and a lack of fear of the LORD. That is, if one thinks that death is all there is and one doesn't expect that there will be any punishment beyond death, why not try to get away with it? Why not try to use your power and to use what tricks and what resources and what cleverness you have? If you succeed, you'll enjoy yourself now and there's nothing particularly that you have need to fear. Let's read a little bit and this comes here from chapter 2 beginning right at verse 1:

> For they reasoned unsoundly, saying to themselves: "Short and sorrowful is our life, and there is no remedy when a man comes to his end, and no one has been known to return from

Hades. Because we were born by mere chance, and hereafter we shall be as though we had never been; because the breath in our nostrils is smoke, and reason is a spark kindled by the beating of our hearts. When it is extinguished, the body will turn to ashes, and the spirit will dissolve like empty air … For our allotted time is the passing of a shadow, and there is no return from our death, because it is sealed up and no one turns back."

Now one hears in a text like that all sorts of references to what happens after death and yet the impression that one gets, here in the reasoning of the ungodly, is that they go to Hades, but there's really no more existence there; one never comes back. Simply everybody goes there and it's dark and dingy and damp and dirty and there's nothing more there. Hence, why not seek to try to make an account of oneself and try to prosper in life now?

Well, in pondering that content, that is the psychology of these wicked men, we might well think that there is actually a philosophical basis for it and I think we'd be right. Materialism is not just a modern invention, granting that there are lots of materialists now, but there were ancient versions of it. In substance, this is, I think, this is the position of Epicurean philosophy. And I think we would do well to pause for a minute and just reflect on the fact that the book the Wisdom of Solomon is bringing into its text a kind of philosophy, a pagan philosophy with which it violently disagrees and it wants to present this as a recipe for disaster. Sometimes the Epicureans are portrayed and dismissed as pure hedonists. Now, as a philosopher and one intent upon the history of philosophy, that would be an unfair judgment. The texts of Epicurus and his followers, in fact, make very sophisticated discriminations about these things. That is, they weigh the different kinds of pleasure. They weigh the intensity of pleasure. They weigh the duration of pleasure and the types of pleasure, but it is a sophisticated position. But even amid its vast sophistication, at the core of the Epicurean position, is precisely the kind of godlessness that the Wisdom of Solomon is here addressing and critiquing. It was Epicurus's view, historically— and we still have the text to prove it—it was Epicurus's view that to be rid of pain, one should include in one's project being rid of the pain of unnecessary fears. And if one wants to be rid of unnecessary fears, one of the things that he thinks we should rid ourselves of is the illusion that there is a God and the illusion that there is an afterlife. Let me quote a short passage from Epicurus. This is found in a very famous letter that he wrote, it's called the Letter to Menoeceus, at paragraph 125, and I'll just read a sentence: "Death … is nothing to us, since so long as we exist, death is not with us; but when death comes, then we do not exist."

Now that's a very interesting piece of logic, isn't it? That is, while we're alive there is no such thing as death and when death comes, we won't be alive. So what is there to fear? We should live while we're living and once we're dead, there's nothing else anyway. Well, he used reasoning like that to try to get people to understand there's nothing to fear in death. There's no reason to think that there's an afterlife. In other texts, he had tried to make his arguments against the existence of God and so he really does have the godlessness and the sense that there's no afterlife that, I think, this book is critiquing.

In setting forth the Epicurean reasoning and the reasoning of the godless here, the text portrays someone who is nonetheless still thinking in some biblical categories. That is, it's not showing us a pure pagan. It's showing us someone who understands the biblical categories, who's still using their terminology even though he's holding that position. Hence, in the passage from the Wisdom of Solomon that I read, we still hear categories like creation, righteousness and sin, even while the person who is saying this speech, namely the wicked that the author of the Wisdom of Solomon is trying to portray, even though the person is taking a position diametrically opposed to the Bible, it's still said in biblical terms. Let me read this time from the middle of chapter 2:

> Come, therefore, let us enjoy the good things that exist, and make use of the creation to the full as in youth … Let us oppress the righteous poor man; let us not spare the widow nor regard the gray hairs of the aged. But let our might be our law of right, for what is weak proves itself to be useless. Let us lie in wait for the righteous man, because he is inconvenient to us and opposes our actions; he reproaches us for sins against the law, and accuses us of sins against our training.

Now in a passage like that, one of course hears those biblical categories I was speaking of. This is part of what makes me think that the situation that we're envisioning are those good and faithful Jews who had to contend with some Jews who were very deeply embracing the Hellenism in Alexandria or in other parts of the ancient world where Roman Hellenism was taking root and was having such a predominant effect. Hence, I think he puts very, very nicely in the psychology of somebody who knows the Bible but is ceasing to accept it.

In any case, what we see in that passage is this: blinded by their own wickedness—that's chapter 2, verse 21—blinded by their wickedness, the speakers devise a plot to see if these righteous Jews, the ones who are still faithful to Torah, see if they will hold fast to their end, see if they'll last in their righteousness. The narrator breaks in a little bit and so after the quotation of the wicked themselves, the narrator comments on specifically what they failed to understand. Namely, they failed to understand what the immortal God intended when creating humankind in those stories of Genesis that they all knew. These comments do not so much assert that human beings are immortal by nature, in a way, say, that a Plato would've argued, but rather, that life without end is a gift that God intends for the virtuous and the righteous. In that previous text that I just read, one even heard some of the words that Plato had put in the mouth of Thrasymachus, "might makes right." That too, I suspect, is part of the philosophical position that is being opposed here, but let's listen again to the narrator in this part of the text. This is chapter 2 beginning at verse 22:

> They did not know the secret purposes of God,
> nor hope for the wages of holiness,
> nor discern the prize for blameless souls;
> for God created man for incorruption,
> and made him in the image of his own eternity,
> but through the devil's envy death entered the world,
> and those who belong to his party experience it.

In that text, we hear one of the really important words of this book, he made them for "incorruption." That is, it's a description already of the fact that God wanted people to live in righteousness so that he could bestow upon them a body that would never corrupt, that would never die, a body that would never fall apart. He intended them for an eternal life in a bodily way. In this comment, the author seems to me very clearly to be alluding to Genesis and specifically to that passage in Genesis in which God has created human beings, male and female, in his own image and likeness. That of course, that phrase, is of such enormous magnitude in subsequent theology when Christians like Augustine will see in that notion of the image and likeness of God, the way we're made. What he thinks happens with original sin, is that image and likeness have been shattered. That they been so very badly wounded.

Of special interest here is the idea of incorruption and later, we're going to see the term immortality. It's like the idea that's found in the book of Ezekiel. If you were to turn to chapter 18, verse 32 or a little bit later on in Ezekiel 33:11, one likewise sees this word showing up, namely that human nature is made for incorruption. The word that's used here in the Greek text of the Wisdom of Solomon is a word that's very familiar from the Greek tradition of philosophy, *aptharsia*. For the first time in the Bible, it occurs here. That is, we had references to the doctrine in Ezekiel but here we're seeing the word and we have an identification of the devil for the very first time, with the serpent mentioned in Genesis. It's a long-standing tradition to interpret that way, that what that serpent was that's described in those earlier chapters tempting Adam and Eve was the devil. This is the first biblical text that actually makes that connection explicitly.

Let's turn now to the next portion of the text beginning at chapter 3 and going to chapter 4, verse 19. This is a part of this opening story that deals with the suffering and the death of the righteous. Chapter 3 and most of chapter 4 offer a wisdom perspective on the problem of innocent suffering by treating them very directly from a divine perspective. Let me read here the first four verses of chapter 3:

> But the souls of the righteous are in the hand of God,
> and no torment will ever touch them.
> In the eyes of the foolish they seem to have died,
> and their departure was thought to be an affliction,
> and their going from us to be their destruction;
> but they are at peace.
> For though in the sight of men they were punished,
> their hope is full of immortality.

Those are words which are now speaking the doctrine of immortality that I have been talking about all the way through this lecture course as where the biblical wisdom tradition ends up on this problem of, how do you deal with the retribution question. Like Sirach, the Wisdom of Solomon can very well envision that suffering may well be a device to test us, to purify us, perhaps to stretch our characters. Some Christians have applied the lines that I just now read to the doctrine of purgatory, that is to that state after death when souls who are not yet ready to see God in heaven are completely purified, where there's a purgation. In that sense, it's not only after death but even earthly trials which can help to purify us. Don't we sometimes know? Let's listen, yet again, to some of the text here that suggested that doctrine to Christians but that is found here in this text of the Wisdom of Solomon already before Christianity. I'm reading verses 5 and 6 from chapter 3:

> Having been disciplined a little, they will receive great good,
> because God tested them and found them worthy of himself;
> like gold in the furnace he tried them,
> and like a sacrificial offering he accepted them.

Within this section then, the text addresses some especially hard cases. It talks about the barren woman, who has no children. It talks about the eunuch, who can have no children. It talks about those who die young. All of these are cases where one cannot make the claim that they will have immortality in their children or that they will be somehow blessed because of their later family. It calls them blessed and does so in direct contrast to the wicked, the adulterers, in the particular case here in chapter 3, verse 10 and following, the adulterers who have lots of children and who may live a long time. That even these sad cases will be blessed because they will have an immortal life that is God's gift to them.

Throughout this material, the author seems to me to be keeping our focus on the moral psychology. That is, on trying to explain how it is that any of us deliberate about moral questions and how we ever come to make the decisions that we do on those questions, as when he notes at the end in one of those last lines, "For the fascination of wickedness obscures what is good, and roving desires pervert the innocent mind." He's got that strong sense of the need to do moral psychology.

Finally, in the passage that goes from chapter 4, verse 20 through chapter 5, verse 23, the author turns to the judgment of the righteous upon the godless, as well as God's justice. The story has a dramatic surprise and it comes in this scene, namely, a scene that is set after the death of both the good and the wicked; suddenly their roles get reversed. Those who were the persecuted now become the judges of their persecutors. Let's read a little bit here from that next passage. It's chapter, 4 verse 20:

> They will come with dread when their sins are reckoned up,
> and their lawless deeds will convict them to their face.
> Then the righteous man will stand with great confidence
> in the presence of those who have afflicted him,
> and those who make light of his labors.
> When they see him, they will be shaken with dreadful fear,
> and they will be amazed at his unexpected salvation.

Much of chapter 5 is then given to the astonished voices of the evildoers who were speaking just a few minutes ago. Earlier on, we quoted them when they were still alive. Let me quote a little bit from the beginning of chapter 5:

> This is the man whom we once held in derision
> and made a byword of reproach—we fools!
> We thought that his life was madness and that his end was
>   without honor.
> Why has he been numbered among the sons of God?
> And why is his lot among the saints?
> What has our arrogance profited us?
> And what good has our boasted wealth brought us?
> All those things have vanished like a shadow,
> and like a rumor that passes us by.

Well after the voices of the wicked have been heard, we now turn to the narrator and the narrator explains the results, not in some philosophical argumentation like Plato's about natural immortality, but in the distinctive approach of the book of Wisdom, namely as a gift that God gives to those who observe his commands and honor his will; chapter 5, verse 15:

> But the righteous live for ever,
> and their reward is with the LORD;
> the Most High takes care of them.
> Therefore they will receive a glorious crown
> and a beautiful diadem from the hand of the LORD,
> because with his right hand he will cover them,
> and with his arm he will shield them.

I stress here the difference between the approach to the question of immortality that Greek philosophy takes and the approach taken here, simply because some readers of this text have interpreted this book as if it were not sufficiently biblical or were too much indebted to Greek philosophy. In my judgment, yes, it does take up some of the concerns of Greek philosophy. I was pointing out, for instance, the Epicureanism that it criticizes as well as some of the vocabulary, whether immortality, *athanasia* in Greek, incorruptibility, *aphtharsia*. But as our own further study will continue to show, this book clearly adapts the meaning of the terms that it's borrowed from Hellenistic philosophy for its own purposes, because I think this book is guided by the inspiration of God who is making this revelation.

In the next lecture, we'll then turn to considerations about the author as standing in the persona of Solomon as he addresses his fellow kings of the earth and makes a certain reflection on this story for them.

Lecture Thirty
The Wisdom of Solomon on Prayer

Scope:

In the tradition of biblical wisdom literature, the middle portion of the Wisdom of Solomon has a lovely wisdom poem in chapters 7 and 8. The setting for this poem is a monologue presented by King Solomon to his fellow rulers. He stresses the duty of kings to cultivate wisdom in order to rise to the challenge of their office. To encourage them to take the means necessary to receive and embrace this instruction in wisdom, he recounts his own life story and offers his poem in praise of Wisdom (a personified figure like the one found in Proverbs) as the source of both theoretical knowledge about the world and practical knowledge useful for the problems of life. The ninth chapter provides a lesson for the kings in how to pray for wisdom. This lecture will focus on chapters 6–9 of the text, with particular attention to the interplay of practical and speculative wisdom.

Outline

I.   The structure of the second part of Wisdom (6:1–9:18).

    A. Just as in the opening line (1:1), the author (in the persona of Solomon) again addresses the kings of the earth at the start of the second part of the text. Whether the author had any realistic expectations that such kings would be likely to read the text is unclear.

    B. But for the likely readers of the book among the Jewish community of Alexandria, this might have proven an interesting perspective: what Solomon, their great sage, might have said if given the chance to address an international community.

    C. The structure of this portion of the text.

        1. Solomon's exhortation to his fellows about the need to seek wisdom from God.

        2. His testimony that it was prayer that brought him the wisdom for which he is known.

        3. His poem in praise of Wisdom.

4. Solomon's further testimony about his courtship of Wisdom.

5. His way of modeling for them the prayer they need to make for wisdom.

II. Solomon's exhortation on the need for rulers to seek wisdom from God (6:1–12).

    A. The connection between the story of the first part of the book and the kings who are addressed is clear from the exhortation that opens the second part: Just as those who abused their power in the story, so too any ruler who abuses power can expect to be held to account.

    B. It is not only the general point that anyone and everyone should expect to render an account of himself, although that in itself would presumably be telling.

    C. There is also a claim about what one might want to call the Bible's political philosophy—a claim that has had a long history in subsequent political thought, namely that because all authority derives from God, rulers can expect to be judged by a strict standard.

    D. This assertion need not be thought simply identical with the claim about the divine right of kings championed by absolutist rulers during the early modern period of history.

    E. A more modest but, in my judgment, more promising way to understand the point comes through a distinction between power (the ability to compel) and authority (the moral status of being entrusted with power and being responsible for any use of that power).

III. Solomon's testimony about his own need for prayer (6:13–7:22a).

    A. Besides the reminder that rulers will have to give an account of their stewardship, Solomon spends much time praising the joys of Wisdom and assuring his fellow kings that even a sincere desire for instruction is the beginning of all wisdom, just as keeping the moral law is an assurance of immortality.

    B. The persona of Solomon then presents himself in an extremely humble way, not as naturally wise but as any other mortal, in need of praying for wisdom.

C. Solomon then testifies to loving the pursuit of divine wisdom more than everything else, and he attributes to God everything that he has received, both of a speculative nature about the elements, the seasons, and the stars and about the practical affairs of statecraft.

IV. The wisdom poem (7:22b–8:1).

A. The wisdom poem, like the others in the tradition before it, envisions wisdom as personified and with all lovely qualities—in fact, some 21 of them are listed.

B. Wisdom is the mother of the virtue and righteousness that lead to immortality and stand before the very throne of God.

C. Many Jewish and Christian commentators with a philosophical bent found special attraction in the lines that deal with the pervasiveness of this divine wisdom as that which makes everything about the universe intelligible because of its order.

V. Solomon on the need for courting Wisdom (8:2–21) and his prayer (9:1–18).

A. Using the imagery of marriage, Solomon testifies to his need to court Wisdom as a bride.

B. He then acknowledges that it is she who has made anyone wise and virtuous. Within the following text we see in particular the four cardinal virtues famous from Greek philosophy: self-control (moderation), prudence (practical wisdom), justice (righteousness), and courage (fortitude).

C. How, Solomon reasons, could he not be willing to take whatever means are necessary in order to obtain what he desires?

VI. Solomon's prayer (9:1–18).

A. Mindful that his fellow kings might need instruction in prayer (like the rest of us), Solomon recounts the prayer that he made to God for wisdom.

B. He acknowledges his own lack of wisdom and yet his urgent need for it, especially given the role he is expected to play for his people.

C. He then praises the wisdom that dwells with God and pleads to be given this gift. One can hear some of the same thoughts that made up the speeches and counterspeeches in Job, but here they are simply put in the service of prayer.

VII. In the following lecture we will examine the final portion of the book, a scriptural illustration from the events of Exodus about the points that Solomon has been making at the general level in his address to his fellow kings.

Suggested Reading:

Collins, *Jewish Wisdom*, 133–57, 178–221.

Duggan, *The Consuming Fire*, 564–81.

Questions to Consider:

1. What do you understand to be the difference between power and authority? Can you think of some examples? What would happen if there were no such distinction, that is, if all authority were merely power?

2. On the basis of what the figure of Solomon says in this part of Wisdom, what are the main duties and responsibilities of a ruler?

3. If you were to compose a prayer for the specific sorts of wisdom that you need, what would you include in your request?

Lecture Thirty—Transcript
The Wisdom of Solomon on Prayer

This lecture will consider the second part of the book called the Wisdom of Solomon, a part that specifically focuses on the need to pray for wisdom. In the tradition of biblical wisdom literature, this middle portion of the book has a lovely wisdom poem that's found in chapters 7 and 8, so much like those earlier wisdom books. But the setting for that wisdom poem is a longer monologue that is presented by the king, Solomon, speaking to his fellow rulers of the earth. He stresses the duty of kings to cultivate wisdom, precisely in order to rise to the challenge of their office, to encourage them to take the means that are necessary to receive and to embrace the instruction and wisdom. He recounts his own life story and he offers his poem, then, in praise of wisdom, telling about wisdom as the source of the theoretical knowledge that he has about the world, as well as the practical knowledge that he has gained that is so useful for all the problems of life, including what he experiences as a king. And then the ninth chapter provides a lesson for them all in how to pray for wisdom. Hence, this lecture will focus on chapters 6 to chapter 9 of the text with particular attention to this interplay between practical and speculative wisdom.

Let's begin then right at chapter 6, and I think it might be helpful just to take a moment to look at the structure of this second part precisely to appreciate how that great wisdom poem sounds. Again, it's the figure of Solomon here, just as it was in the opening line, chapter 1, verse 1. So too, the author is taking a persona, namely the persona of King Solomon and as in the beginning, so too, here again at chapter 6, he addresses the kings of the earth. It's as though they were all somehow gathered together here at the start of the second part of the text. Whether the author had any realistic expectation that anybody else besides the Jewish community would ever read this is unclear, but he takes that as the scenario. For those likely readers of this book, whom I presume to be among the Jewish community at Alexandria, I think this might prove to be a very interesting perspective—what their great sage, King Solomon, might have said if he had been given the chance to address the international community. In any case, it still summons our attention.

Let's look then at the structure of this second part of the book. First, we have Solomon's exhortation to his fellow kings about the need to seek wisdom from God and not to simply be reliant upon their own wits or upon their own studies or upon their own two cents; that's chapter 6, verses 1–12. Then beginning at chapter 6, verse 13 and going up through the middle of chapter 7, is a second part, namely Solomon's testimony that it was prayer that brought him the wisdom for which he is known—and one thinks about all the other stories about Solomon that we examined earlier in this course. The third part, beginning at verse 22 of chapter 7 through the beginning of chapter 8, is a poem in praise of wisdom and it's so very much resonant with the echoes of what we saw in those earlier wisdom poems when we looked at them earlier in our lecture series. The fourth part begins at verse 2 of chapter 8 and goes to verse 21. It's Solomon giving testimony to those fellow kings about his own life story. He does it in the marital imagery of courtship, that wisdom was a lady that he had to court. Finally, the fifth part, and that's the whole of chapter 9. It's his way of modeling for them. That is, he wants to teach them not only about wisdom, but even how to do the prayer that they need to make and so he exemplifies it with a prayer of his own that constitutes chapter 9.

Let's turn then to the beginning of this here, right at the start of chapter 6, where Solomon is exhorting his fellow kings on the need to seek wisdom from God rather than just depend upon themselves. We see right here at the beginning of chapter 6, a relation to the previous story that had been told in chapters 1–5 and that we examined in the last lecture. The connection between the story that's told in the first part and the kings who are now being addressed by Solomon becomes clear from the exhortation right at the start of chapter 6. Namely, just as those people in the story who abused their power, so too any ruler who abuses his power can be expected to be held to account. Those wicked people were held to account, so too a king who is wicked will be held to account. It's not just the general point that anyone and everyone should expect to render an account of himself—although even if it were that general point that would presumably be telling—but this is specifically about kings. He wants them to know that they are also subject to this sort of reckoning.

It strikes me that as he starts to make his case for that, what we get here is a kind of political philosophy. You could call it the Bible's political philosophy. There is a claim about what it is that is the source and justification for power. This, of course, had a long history within subsequent political thought. It's the notion, and you see it at least hints of it here, that gets developed in the subsequent tradition. Because all authority derives from God, rulers can expect to be judged not just by a normal standard but by a very strict standard. God has given them the power. God will test them on how well they used it.

Presumably, the second part here follows quite directly and immediately from the first and it's in that spirit, that direct connection, that we get not only the exhortations still echoing in our ears but we get a very strong and controversial claim. Let me read a little bit here from chapter 6:

> Give ear, you that rule over multitudes, and boast of many nations.
> For your dominion was given you from the LORD,
> and your sovereignty from the Most High,
> who will search out your works and inquire into your plans.

When putting the matter like that, Solomon is stating to them clearly, there's a high level of expectation. The assertion need not be thought of as exactly identical with what later politically philosophy does with it, even though there is a strong claim that they've gotten their power from God. Later on, in this tradition of political philosophy, one will hear, for instance in the early modern period of history, what's called the divine right of kings. That was a political philosophy that was championed by those absolutist rulers in the modern period, people like the British monarchs, James I, Charles I, Charles II. They did it not only in the way they conducted themselves in office, but theoretically in some books, James I, for instance, wrote a book called *Defense of the Right of Kings*, where he claimed this absolute power.

One might, I suppose, even hear some of the much more modest medieval theories which held that monarchs are God's vice regents on earth but somehow in a relationship that's complicated, but parallel to the church. Those medieval authors and the British monarchs liked to invoke the Bible in justifying their own claim. One can still see some of this in the vestiges of the consecration ceremonies, the very formal rights that are used with some monarchs today and that tended to be derived from the way in which the coronation of the Holy Roman Emperor took place.

Both in those rights and in these theoretical defenses, those monarchs try to use scriptural passages. They sometimes invoke this one that we just read from the book of Wisdom, just as they sometimes use passages from the book of Romans, the letter of St. Paul to the Romans, chapter 13. One sees this for instance, in a book Sir Robert Filmer wrote, called *Patriarchia*, back in 1680. They use arguments that are both scriptural and philosophical, but on the other hand, there will be people who will use the same scriptural treatises, the same scriptural references, against those absolutist claims. I think of for instance, Robert Bellarmine in his treatise on civil government or perhaps John Locke in his first treatise on civil government, and they will try to oppose the use of these biblical texts because they're not making the claims that the absolute monarchs like to make.

If any of the monarchists might have had the ability to make such a claim about a direct divine appointment, it would presumably have been the kings of ancient Israel. They were really given their power directly by God. The claims that these kings in the modern period make to that same sort of appointment do not seem to have stood the test of time, if they're judged even plausibly at all, but some of them rely on these texts.

A much more modest way of doing this, and in my judgment, a much more promising way to understand the point, comes through a philosophical distinction I'd like to propose to you, namely, a distinction between power and authority. I think of power as force; the ability to compel somebody. On the other hand, I think of authority as not just power but rather, a moral status, a matter of being entrusted with power and then being responsible for any use one makes of that power. Unless one grants some kind of distinction—whatever words you use—unless you grant some kind of distinction between power, that is force and authority, the moral witness, the moral use one must make of the power one has been entrusted—unless one makes some sort of distinction along these general lines, I think that there is going to be no relevant difference between the way a thief uses force and the way a police officer uses force when collaring the thief. That is, the police officer has a certain moral authority for the use of power, which the thief does not. The police do not have carte blanche permission simply to use force, but rather they have to be restrained in their use of force by the protocols that have been established by some higher authority yet, ultimately a city government or a state government who are acting in service of the common good. By contrast, thieves operate without any such moral authority, rather along the very lines that the Wisdom of Solomon, back in chapter 2 at verse 11, had indicated. They operate only on the philosophy that might makes right, that their power gives them whatever authority they're claiming. Hence, I would suggest what we have here in terms of a biblical philosophy or a biblical political philosophy is not the absolutist claim to power that some of those monarchs made, but rather a very sensible distinction between power and authority. When it's applied to the present case, this distinction between power and authority would mean that rulers, kings in Solomon's day—we might think of presidents or prime ministers or any other office you might care to think of—that these people have authority and that they are authorities who have been entrusted with various powers. It is not that God directly appoints them, maybe the kings of Israel could make that claim. It's not necessarily that God has directly appointed all these other kings to whom Solomon is speaking, but rather that even these kings, however they got their authority, whether they were Roman or Greek or anywhere else in the ancient world, however they got their authority, they are morally responsible to this higher authority that is God. They're responsible for the ways in which they use the powers at their disposal. I think that's the case that King Solomon is here making.

What he does with it, is start to give them some testimony. That is, he puts himself as an equal, on par with the rest of them and he want to suggests, just as in his case, so too in their case, they need to pray for wisdom just as he needed to pray for wisdom. This is the section that begins at chapter 6, verse 13 and goes through chapter 7, verse 22. I'd like to think of this along the lines of that old maxim, one attracts more bees with honey than with vinegar. He's going to try to attract them in that same way. Besides the reminder that he gives them, that rulers will have to give an account of their stewardship, Solomon spends a lot of time praising the joys of wisdom—that's verses 12–25 of chapter 6—and assuring his fellow kings that even a sincere desire for instruction is the beginning of wisdom. How many times did we see that in earlier parts of biblical wisdom literature? That's chapter 6, verse 17. Likewise he tells them that keeping the laws of wisdom is an assurance of immortality. Again, we're picking up on that theme of immortality as we saw in the first five chapters.

The persona of Solomon here, this king addressing his fellow kings. He presents himself to his fellow kings in an extremely humble way, not as someone who is naturally wise, but as a man, just like any other mortal man, someone who is in need of acquiring wisdom and who knows that he needs to pray for it. In passing, one can see in the text that I'm going to read now the typical Hebrew manner of counting that differs a little bit from our own way of counting. It includes the first and the last within the series just a little bit differently but it's interesting to note how that text works. I'll read then from chapter 7:

> I also am mortal, like all men,
> a descendant of the first formed child of the earth;
> and in the womb of a mother I was molded into flesh
> within the period of ten months, compacted with blood,
> from the seed of a man and the pleasure of marriage. ...
> For no king has had a different beginning of existence;
> there is for all mankind one entrance into life, and a
>   common departure.
> Therefore I prayed, and understanding was given me.
> I called upon God, and the spirit of wisdom came to me. ...

We see that point about counting, that he calls it ten months within the womb. Well it's not that they thought it lasted 10 months but that they have a slightly different way of doing their counting. But most importantly, he's appealing to the kings of earth, I'm a mortal just like you. He does it by telling them of how he was conceived, that he's just a man like any other, but then, he tells them and he testifies to the fact that he prayed and wisdom was given him. He testifies to the fact that he had to lovingly pursue wisdom and he had to pursue wisdom more than he pursued anything else in life. He attributes to God everything that he has received of wisdom.

This is interesting, I think, that it's not only that he received the practical part of wisdom, but the speculative part of wisdom, as he's going to say in the things that come next. He receives speculative wisdom about nature, about the elements, about the seasons, about the stars. And likewise, he received what he considers to be so deeply important, a wisdom about the practical affairs of statecraft: how one should deliberate, how one should make decisions, how one should try to be just, how one should accomplish all the tasks that are given to a king.

The next portion of the book is different. This is where Solomon breaks into praise. In particular, it's a poem that's in the tradition of the great wisdom poems. We begin at chapter 7, verse 22 and it goes to chapter 8, verse 1. In this wisdom poem, as in the other wisdom poems in the tradition before it, what we see is Wisdom personified. She has all the lovely qualities just as Lady Wisdom did in the book of Proverbs or that we saw in the tradition of Sirach. Here, in fact, there are some 21 qualities that are listed. The Wisdom of Solomon likes to articulate things and to make all sorts of distinctions. She has 21 lovely qualities and here she is taken—in this passage that I'll read right now—she's taken as the mother of virtue and the mother of righteousness, those qualities of a moral character that lead to immortality and that stand before the very throne of God. I suspect we're seeing already the connection between this part of the book and the previous part of the book. Hence, reading beginning at chapter 7, verse 25:

> For she is a breath of the power of God,
> and a pure emanation of the glory of the Almighty;
> therefore nothing defiled gains entrance into her.
> For she is a reflection of eternal light,
> a spotless mirror of the working of God,
> and an image of his goodness.
> Though she is but one, she can do all things,
> and while remaining in herself, she renews all things;
> in every generation she passes into holy souls
> and makes them friends of God, and prophets;
> for God loves nothing so much as the man who lives
> with wisdom. …

One hears in that text all sorts of interesting connections. One hears for instance at the very beginning of it, that theme of breath that we were commenting on earlier when we were noticing the connection between breath and the soul as well as breath and the spirit. Many Jewish and Christian commentators who have a bit of a philosophical bent have found special attraction in the lines that we just read that deal with the pervasiveness of this divine wisdom, that which makes everything about the whole universe intelligible, able to be understood precisely because of its order. I think you see that especially in chapter 8, verse 1 which reads as follows, "She reaches mightily from one end of the earth to the other, and she orders all things well." In that passage, as well as in the reflection on it, that notion of ordering. One will see Augustine, for instance, using it. One will see heavy use of it in the tradition of Maimonides. Ordering all things well is the way in which God has intervened by his providence and created a world that is deeply orderly and that can give us a deeper understanding of the Creator by appreciating the order that is within creation.

Let's turn now to the next part of this. That is beginning at chapter 8, verse 2, and what we hear is Solomon on the need to pay court to Wisdom. He uses marital imagery for this, and then in chapter 9, we'll see his prayer, but first this marital imagery and the courtship tradition. Using the imagery of marriage, something of course we've seen repeatedly in the wisdom literature tradition, Solomon testifies to his need to court her as a bride. That is, he can't simply expect that this is given to him, rather, he has to work at it. There's a gift awaiting him but he's got to have enough energy and enough fidelity and enough perseverance as a young man courting his bride; verse 2 and 3 of chapter 8:

> I loved her and sought her from my youth,
> and I desired to take her for my bride,
> and I became enamored of her beauty.
> She glorifies her noble birth by living with God,
> and the LORD of all loves her. ...

One sees in that marital imagery, I think an echo of what we saw in the Song of Songs where that marital imagery was used in the wisdom literature tradition to talk about the way in which this courtship and this marriage would eventually be made. Here in this text, the next thing he'll do is to acknowledge that it is Lady Wisdom, it is Wisdom herself, who has made anyone wise and virtuous who has wisdom and virtue. In the next text that I'd like to read for you, we see yet another hint of this philosophical tradition, the borrowing from Greek philosophy when the text is ready to borrow it and I just think this is so significant. That is, it's not that Greek philosophy is controlling the biblical text, but rather, that the author, the biblical author can use Greek philosophy.

In the last lecture we saw the author use it to criticize Epicureanism and to criticize one of the same things that Plato criticized, that "might makes right" tradition. Here in this next text, the author borrows the four cardinal virtues that are absolutely famous from Greek philosophy: first, self-control or moderation; secondly, prudence in the sense of practical wisdom, the ability to make good deliberation and good judgments; third, justice or righteousness. I think more often in the Hebrew tradition it's called righteousness. In the Greek tradition there's this long standing interest in justice, *diakaiosune* that Plato and Aristotle had discussed; and fourthly, courage or fortitude. One finds it here in this text that comes from chapter 8 beginning at verse 7:

> And if any one loves righteousness, her labors are virtues;
> for she teaches self-control and prudence, justice, and
>   courage. ...
> And if anyone longs for wide experience,
> she knows the things of old and infers the things to come;
> she understands turns of speech and the solution of riddles;
> she has foreknowledge of signs and wonders
> and of the outcomes of seasons and times. ...

One sees there very clearly the use of this four-fold tradition of the virtues as well as indications about some of the other things one would expect in the wisdom tradition, philosophical or biblical.

Solomon goes on; how, Solomon, reasons, how could he not be willing to take whatever means was necessary in order to obtain something so beautiful, something that he so much desires? I'll continue then at chapter 8, verse 17:

> When I considered these things inwardly,
> and thought upon them in my mind,
> that in kinship with wisdom there is immortality,
> and in friendship with her, pure delight,
> and in the labor of her hands, unfailing wealth,
> and in the experience of her company, understanding,
> and renown in sharing her words,
> I went about seeking how to get her for myself. ...
> But I perceived that I would not possess wisdom
> unless God gave her to me—
> and it was a mark of insight to know whose gift she was—
> so I appealed to the LORD and besought him,
> and with my whole heart I said. ...

And then he goes on. We'll hear next the prayer that he goes on to. I would urge you though, in hearing words like this to remember the imagined scenario. He's talking to his fellow kings of the earth and kings of the earth, some of them, especially the more studious ones, know how much effort they had to put in to try to get the wisdom they needed to govern. Some of them, of course, may be proud or arrogant; they may be like some of the wicked people whom Solomon has described early on in the text that we discussed in the previous lecture. They may be ready to leave this to their courtiers because some kings get, they amass, a group of learned men who can perhaps give them guidance which sometimes they'll take and sometimes they will not. Solomon is trying to make an impression on them, namely, that he needed, in his own personal experience, to seek wisdom with all his might and then to pray for it.

Well, mindful that his fellow kings might well need some instruction in prayer like the rest of us, Solomon then recounts the specific prayer that he made to God for wisdom. He wants to tell them not only in an abstract way that they need to pray but he wants to exemplify it for them. In the prayer that he says, this is chapter 9, he first begins by praising God for his mercy. That, of course, is such a deep element of the Jewish tradition, the notion that God is ultimately steadfast in his love and deeply merciful. So he praises God for his mercy and then proceeds to beg God for the gift of wisdom. He tells God in the course of this prayer, we're up to chapter 9 verse 5, he acknowledges his own lack of wisdom and he expresses his urgent need for it, especially given the role that he is expected to play for his people. It's not just for himself that he wants this, but for the people whom he must govern. Then, beginning at chapter 9, verse 9, he praises the wisdom that dwells with God and he pleads to be given this gift. One can hear some of the same thoughts that made up the speeches and the counter-speeches in Job, when we were looking at the way in which that discussion went on, but here they are simply put in the service of prayer. Let me recite, just a couple of lines from that prayer. I'll start at chapter 9, verse 10:

> Send her forth from the holy heavens,
> and from the throne of thy glory send her,
> that she may be with me and toil,
> and that I may learn what is pleasing to thee.
> For she knows and understands all things,
> and she will guide me wisely in my actions
> and guard me with her glory.
> Then my works will be acceptable,
> and I shall judge thy people justly,

and shall be worthy of the throne of my father.
And what man can learn the counsel of God?
Or who can discern what the LORD wills?
For the reasoning of mortals is worthless,
and our designs are likely to fail,
for a perishable body weighs down the soul,
and this earthly tent burdens the thoughtful mind. ...

When Solomon says lines like that, again, one hears a bit of Job and his friends, one hears many echoes from the biblical wisdom literature tradition that he all packs together in this prayer that he's using to exemplify to his fellow kings of the earth.

In the next lecture, we'll examine the final portion of this book from chapters 10–19. What's contained there, what you'll find if you read it ahead of time, is a scriptural illustration that King Solomon wants to give to his fellow kings of the earth. He's going to tell them about events from Exodus. He's going to try to exemplify for them points from the history of how this worked in Israel, as a way for them to understand how perhaps this has worked in the history of their own people.

Lecture Thirty-One
The Wisdom of Solomon on Divine Providence

Scope:

The third portion of the Wisdom of Solomon (chapters 10 to 19) adopts a strategy similar to the last portion of Sirach with its attention to the proactive role of God's providential wisdom in the history of the chosen people. This lecture will focus on four elements that are distinctive in this book: (1) the use of a certain amount of Greek philosophy within a biblical text, (2) the parallels between this book's account of biblical history and the philosophical tradition of natural law ethics, (3) the use of satire (chapters 13 to 15) to ridicule the folly involved in idolatry, and (4) the intimations of a doctrine of resurrection of the body within the book's teachings on the immortality of the soul.

Outline

I. The final section of Wisdom (10:1–19:22).

  A. The contrast between the righteous and the godless in the chapters that open the book is picked up again in the contrast between Israel and Egypt in the time of Moses and the covenant.

  B. If we bear in mind the focus throughout the Wisdom of Solomon on the plight of Alexandrian Jews who might be susceptible to the forces of Hellenistic culture, it will readily become clear that the elaborate account of the struggle between Israel and Egypt from Exodus being retold here really pertains to the Jewish community in Diaspora.

  C. The idolatry of the Egyptians at the time of Moses as described here bears more than a passing resemblance to the orgiastic mystery cults of Dionysus typical of the Roman Empire in the Hellenistic period.

  D. The structure of this material is somewhat complex: a narration of the history of God's chosen people, with special emphasis on a series of comparisons between Israel and Egypt, plus two lengthy meditations.

II. From Creation to the Exodus (10:1–11:14).

    A. Without mentioning any names, the 10th chapter of Wisdom briefly recounts a series of stories from Genesis and Exodus that would easily be recognizable to the Jews in Diaspora at Alexandria. Each story emphasizes the saving work of wisdom.

    B. Just in case the lesson might be lost by this speedy review of events from early in the Bible, the text pauses to draw the lesson.

    C. In the extended treatment between Israel and Egypt, there is not only a contrast between the righteous and the unrighteous but also in the way the same natural element is used for salvation and destruction.

    D. Here the author announces the theme and then exemplifies it by contrasting the first of the plagues, the waters of the Nile that become filled with blood (according to Exodus 7), with the water that God provided to Israel in the desert.

III. A meditation on divine power and mercy (11:15–12:27).

    A. The address shifts from the kings, who are supposed to listen to these stories, to God himself, who is addressed directly and praised for his goodness. This section seems to be the voice of the Wisdom of Solomon in the long-standing debate within wisdom literature about the goodness and power of God.

    B. With the support of allusions to a grand variety of passages from Torah, the author acknowledges the purpose of displays of divine power.

    C. In lines like these, we see the author's deep-seated perspective about the goodness of creation and God's readiness to spare not only Israel (12:12–22) but also her enemies, if only they would repent, as in the sections devoted to the Canaanites (12:3–11) and Egyptians (12:13–27).

IV. Meditation on the temptations to idolatry (13:1–15:19).

    A. From a relatively specific mention of Egyptian idolatry, the author turns to a more general critique of idolatry, beginning with various forms of nature worship.

B. Even apart from divine revelation, one should be able to know enough about the existence of God and the need to worship God as the author of nature rather than to worship nature itself.

C. While the author cannot dismiss this confusion between creature and Creator, he finds it less blameworthy than those who make idols for themselves.

D. Pagan rituals turn into their own punishments: People devoting themselves to their passions stifle even the slightest inclination toward holiness and eternal life.

E. As in the opening portion of the book, there are several allusions to immortality in the final portion of the book.

V. The plagues of Egypt (16:1–19:22).

A. The final section of the text continues with the series of contrasts between the righteous (those who have kept the commandments) and the ungodly (those who have violated the commandments).

B. They are organized on the same model as the author's contrast of water and blood in chapter 11, by listing the ways in which divine wisdom used similar elements from nature for the salvation of Israel and the destruction of the Egyptians.

C. After this dramatically recounted set of comparisons, the book ends in simple praise.

VI. As in Sirach, what is most prominent in wisdom literature of this sort is memory: Wisdom is a matter of keeping present to one's mind the covenant and the promises.

A. The Wisdom of Solomon as a whole thus combines some of the prominent approaches to wisdom that we have seen before. In the cultivation of historical memory, the book functions like Proverbs and Sirach to exhort us with the prospect of divine intervention on behalf of the just.

B. In the meantime, the counsel of the Wisdom of Solomon is fidelity in prayer, so in the next lecture we will turn once again to the Psalms.

Suggested Reading:

Duggan, *The Consuming Fire*, 564–82.

Leaney, *The Jewish and Christian World 200 B.C. to A.D. 200*.

Questions to Consider:

1. How is the attack on idolatry in Wisdom of Solomon related to the concerns of the Torah? What factors in the historical situation prompted this renewal of emphasis?

2. According to Wisdom, what effect does idolatry have on the worshiper? How does the text try to warn believers against these practices? What parallels are there today?

3. What purpose does the review of historical events from Exodus serve in the book of Wisdom? What is the significance of telling Israel's stories without naming the individuals who played great roles in that history? Why the concentration on each of the plagues?

Lecture Thirty-One—Transcript
The Wisdom of Solomon on Divine Providence

This lecture concerns the third and final portion of the book the Wisdom of Solomon, that is, the part from chapter 10 through chapter 19. This third portion adopts a strategy quite similar to the strategy we saw in the last portion of the book of Sirach, precisely by its attention to the proactive role of God's providential wisdom within the history of the Chosen People. In this lecture, what I'll concentrate on is four things, four elements that are very distinctive of this book: first, the use of a certain amount of Greek philosophy within a biblical text; second, the parallels between this book's account of biblical history and a philosophical tradition called natural law ethics; third, the use of satire, that's especially found in chapters 13 to 15, where the book uses satire to ridicule the folly that's involved in idolatry ; and fourth, the intimations of a doctrine of resurrection of the body within the teachings of this book on immortality of the soul.

Let's begin then with the opening part of this final section of the book of Wisdom; the part as a whole that I'm covering is chapter 10 to chapter 19, but to look especially at that opening segment. There is a contrast, here again, just as we saw in the beginning of the book of Solomon and as we saw in the book of Proverbs and elsewhere, a contrast between the righteous and the godless. What was present in the opening part of the Wisdom of Solomon is picked up again here. This time, though, the contrast between the righteous and the godless is a contrast between Israel and Egypt in the time of Moses, at the time of the giving of the Great Covenant that is the Decalogue.

If we bear in mind the focus that is present throughout the book, the Wisdom of Solomon—the focus on the plight of the Alexandrian Jews who were susceptible to Hellenistic culture—I think it will become very readily clear that the elaborate account of the struggle between Israel and Egypt that's being retold here from Exodus, in this last section of this book, is really a discussion about the trials and tribulations and temptations that the Jewish community in say the 1st century B.C. is experiencing in Diaspora. It's allegorical, very easily and clearly for them. In this extensive treatment then of stories about how God liberated his people from slavery, we are presented with a view of wisdom not just as responsible for the creation of the world—we saw that earlier in what Solomon had to say—but also a

God responsible for the salvation of Israel in a time of trouble and a time of crisis. One might want to take a look at chapter 9, verse 18 to see the strength of that.

The section that is dedicated to the idolatry of the Egyptians at the time of Moses—we'll see that a little bit later in what we're going to discuss in this lecture—clearly bears more than a passing resemblance to the orgiastic mystery cults of Dionysus typical of the Roman Empire during the Hellenistic period. It will be useful for us here at the beginning of this lecture to consider the structure of this last portion because it's a pretty complex structure. Namely, it's a narration of the history of God's Chosen People, but it's interrupted at some points in order to give special emphasis to some comparisons, to a series of comparisons between Israel and Egypt. And then in addition, there are two relatively lengthy meditations within it, two reflections on the significance of all this history. First part, right at chapter 10, verse 1 through about verse 14 of chapter 11, what we get is an account of the time described earlier in the Bible from the Creation up to the Exodus. There will be an interesting segment, for instance, on how Wisdom uses water to save Israel. The second part is one of these meditations, namely it's a meditation on divine power and mercy. That goes from chapter 11, verse 15 to chapter 12, verse 27 and the author isn't now recounting the history anymore but is reflecting on what we've seen about divine power and mercy in that history. The third part—begins at chapter 13, verse 1 and goes through the end of chapter 15—is a second meditation and it's a meditation on the temptation to idolatry. I think of the author as so really vigorously interested in saving his people from the temptations to idolatry that are found in Alexandria, that he goes back and thinks about the idolatry that was so tempting to Israel earlier on in its history. The fourth part is Wisdom's use of the plagues during Egypt. I mean, it's a very creative use of that part of the Bible. Wisdom is meditating on the plagues of Egypt for the salvation of the righteous and the affliction of their persecutors; that goes from chapter 16 right at the beginning through the end of the book, chapter 19, verse 22.

Let's now take these, each one in turn, beginning with the section on the time from Creation to the Exodus that's found in chapters 10 and 11. What we get here is a series of historical contrasts, but it's done by the figure of Solomon talking to the kings of the earth, and so he does it without mentioning the names. It's almost like the tradition of the everyman tradition, where you don't need to know the names, what you need to get is the lesson, because these other kings of the earth won't even recognize the names. Without mentioning any names, the tenth chapter of Wisdom briefly recounts a series of stories from Genesis and Exodus that would be easily recognizable to the Jews in Diaspora at Alexandria, and each story in the series emphasizes the saving work that God does by his wisdom. For instance, we hear of the grace of wisdom for ruling all the creatures that Adam received after his transgression; that's the very first two verses of chapter 10 and then pretty rapidly, in a series of disasters and the way wisdom rectifies those disasters.

We hear first of the punishment that the unrighteous Cain receives. Cain, of course, had slain his brother, Abel; that's chapter 10, verse 3. Then we hear about the deliverance of the family of Noah. It's pictured in verse 4 as a kind of new creation. At least it's a new chance for humankind because humanity begins again here. Next, we get the dispersal of the human community. This is the story of the Tower of Babel, the multiplication of languages, but at the same time that we're hearing about all of that destruction and all of that separation, very quickly within the same verse, the fifth verse of chapter 10, we get the fortitude that was especially given to Abraham to withstand the challenge. Chapter 10, verses 6 and 7 have that same alternation, the fire and brimstone that is sent upon Sodom and Gomorrah, but then the rescue of the families of Abraham and of Lot.

Well, after the author has had the chance to give this series of stories, very, very quickly—the kings of the earth probably wouldn't recognize the names but Israel in Diaspora would recognize them even without being told these names—then the author meditates on this in order draw out the lesson, just in case the lesson might be lost by so speedy a review of events from early in the Bible. The text pauses to draw the lesson and perhaps we should pause with it and read that passage so as to get the intended implication of all this. I'm reading chapter 10, verses 8 and 9:

> Because they passed wisdom by,
> they not only were hindered from recognizing the good,
> but also left for mankind a reminder of their folly
> so that their failures could never go unnoticed.
> Wisdom rescued from troubles those who served her.

It's a pretty obvious lesson that he draws there, but in drawing it, makes it very clear for those who are recognizing the stories. The historical march then continues rather quickly. We get stories about Jacob and Esau. We get stories about Joseph and his brothers, and then at somewhat greater length, the author slows down this rapid review and dwells on the time of Moses and Pharaoh. I'm up to chapter 10, verses 15–16. We get Moses and Pharaoh. We get the liberation of the people from Egypt, four or five verses, and then, for the first 14 verses of chapter 11, their long sojourn in the desert.

In the extended treatment then, that is given between Israel and Egypt, there is not only a contrast between the righteous and the unrighteous, but also, and very interestingly, in the way in which the same natural element is used for salvation and for destruction. This type of contrast will later on be continued in chapters 16–19 of Wisdom after the author has completed his lengthy meditations on divine power and mercy and his meditation on idolatry, but here, back in chapters 10 and 11, here he announces the theme of how God, through his wisdom, uses this very same element. He announces the theme and then he exemplifies it by starting to go through the plagues, and here we get the first of the plagues described in some detail, namely the waters of the Nile that become filled with blood. This is recounted, for example, in Exodus, chapter 7. That's contrasted with the water that God uses and that God provides to Israel in the desert. So we've got sort of the same element, but being used for very different purposes. Let me read a little bit from chapter 11:

> For through the very things by which their enemies
>   were punished,
> they themselves received benefit in their need.
> Instead of the fountain of an ever-flowing river,
> stirred up and defiled with blood
> in rebuke for the decree to slay the infants,
> thou gavest them abundant water unexpectedly,
> showing by their thirst at that time
> how thou didst punish their enemies.
> For when they were tried, though they were being
>   disciplined in mercy,
> they learned how the ungodly were tormented when judged
>   in wrath.

Again, it's a complicated text but what one sees in that complicated text is the author having meditated on the significance of the way in which God acted in history just as in Sirach; so too here in the Wisdom of Solomon. The author is meditating on history and divine providence is playing a role in history, exhibiting the divine wisdom and the divine power.

The next section begins at chapter 11, verse 15 and goes up to chapter 12, verse 27 and it's, as I said before, a meditation on the power of God and the mercy of God. The address shifts from the kings who are supposed to be listening to these stories, the focus shifts to God himself, because here the author starts addressing God directly and praising God for his goodness. The section, in my judgment, seems to be the very voice of the Wisdom of Solomon in that long-standing debate that we saw and that we studied, especially when we were reviewing the story of the book of Job; namely, a debate within wisdom literature about the goodness and power of God.

With the support of allusions to a great variety of passages from Torah, the author acknowledges the purpose of all these displays of divine power. Let me read just two verses here from chapter 11, right at the beginning of this section, chapter 11, verse 15, and I think you'll see the way in which he's using Torah so carefully: "Thou didst send upon them a multitude of irrational creatures to punish them, / that they might learn that one is punished by the very things by which he sins."

It's an interesting reflection on, sometimes there really will be retribution because God will even use the very nature of the sin to inflict a kind of punishment. Another one of the lines that occurs here that becomes an absolute favorite with later theologians reflecting on this text, is chapter 11, verse 20: "But thou hast arranged all things by measure and number and weight."

Even in that short little verse, that appeal to the orderliness of divine providence and figures like Augustine and Maimonides, Thomas Aquinas, they use this in order to reflect upon the massive organization present in the universe. This is the verse they always cite, right here from the Wisdom of Solomon.

Our author continues by meditating upon the merciful intent of God in all these displays of power. For instance, chapter 11, verse 23 and 24:

> But thou art merciful to all, for thou canst do all things,
> and thou dost overlook men's sins, that they may repent.
> For thou lovest all things that exist, and hast loathing for
> none of the things which thou hast made, for thou
> wouldst not have made anything if thou hadst hated it.

Now what I see in a passage like that, I suspect you do too, is that allusion to what we noticed about the covenant with Noah; namely, that God will overlook sins for awhile and that this is part of the mystery of human beings having freedom; namely, that there will be a consequence for every action in the natural world, but that God allows us the freedom of time; that there's not an immediate retribution for the wicked actions or for the actions that are in any way sinful. But rather, there is an ongoing experience of time in which people can sometimes see the natural consequences of their actions and may choose to repent. We meditated on that considerably ourselves but here we're trying to follow Solomon's meditation.

In lines like these, I think we see the author's deep-seated meditation, his deep-seated perspective about the goodness of creation and about God's readiness to spare not only Israel, that's chapter 12 from about verse 12 to verse 22, but also a willingness to spare Israel's enemies, if only they would repent. One sees that, for instance, in chapter 12, verses 3–11 which are devoted to the Canaanites and then chapter 12, verse 13 up to verse 27, which is explicitly devoted to the Egyptians. God had carried out these punishments against the Egyptians, but did the punishments slowly and gradually and what our author sees as the reason for that slow and gradual infliction of punishment was an effort by God to stir up the consciences of the Egyptians, to stir them up to repentance. Again, part of what I've been trying to argue, you've seen it already, is that this is not just a historical recap on what happened back in Exodus when Moses is describing the actual scenario in history, but this is the author of the Wisdom of Solomon talking to his own people in Alexandria and urging them, they need to reflect on this, they need to make this same meditation.

In chapter 13, we see the author making a second meditation. This time, he's going to focus on this topic of idolatry. It goes from chapter 13, right at the beginning, verse 1, up to chapter 15, verse 19. Idolatry, of course, is the worship of something other than God, the worship of the creature as if it were the Creator; and this part gets highly satirical. From a relatively specific mention of Egyptian idolatry, the author then turns to a much more general critique of any form of idolatry beginning with certain forms of nature worship; that's the first nine verses of chapter 13.

Even apart from divine revelation, the author reasons, one should be able to know enough about the existence of God and the need to worship God as the author of nature rather than ever worshipping nature itself. Let's listen to a couple of those lines. It's a part that begins right at the beginning of chapter 13:

> For all men who were ignorant of God were foolish
>   by nature;
> and they were unable from the good things that are seen to
>   know him who exists,
> nor did they recognize the craftsman while paying heed to
>   his works;
> but they supposed that either fire or wind or swift air, or
>   turbulent water,
> or the luminaries of heaven were the gods that rule
>   the world.

One hears in that passage what the ancients thought of as the four elements as well as that which transcends the elements, the stars, and notices that various peoples, various thinkers have been inclined to worship one or another of those elements as gods. The insights here, in this text, have been a mainstay of much religious philosophy throughout the ages; namely, the insight that even though God is infinite and transcendent and unable to in any way be encompassed within our human categories, one can, nevertheless, and one is expected, nevertheless, to grasp a certain amount of information and wisdom about the cause from knowing the effects that are within our powers of observation. One is culpable for not grasping that the cause had to be at least as powerful as the effects that are produced; hence, for this reason, the author can criticize those who fail to do so. But it's not just that the author criticizes. We also get some of that same moral psychology that I was referring to two lectures ago when I was stressing that even from the beginning of the book, this author is enormously focused on moral psychology, on how we go wrong sometimes in our thinking.

Here, the way it shows up is this: there's a loss of human dignity that can come from worshipping something less than human. While the author cannot dismiss this confusion between creature and Creator, he finds nature worship far less blameworthy than those who actually make idols because when they make the idol, they know in their heart of hearts that what they've made is not a god. This is what's found in chapter 13 beginning around verse 8.

In a very sophisticated move, the author explains that the problem is not that anyone who thinks that the gold and silver or stone or wooden images is God, but rather, that the one who made those images is really corrupting himself, that human dignity will be corrupted by worshipping something that really is merely the product of one's own hands. And then acting with the moral abandon that comes from knowing that there is no god in what I've already myself just made. Again, listen to some of his satire here. I'm in the middle of chapter 13:

> A castoff piece,… useful for nothing, a stick crooked and full of knots,
> he … carves with care in his leisure … he forms it like the image of a man, …
> then he makes for it a niche that befits it,
> and sets it in the wall, and fastens it there with iron.
> So he takes thought for it, that it may not fall,
> because he knows that it cannot help itself,
> for it is only an image and has need of help.

There's a mindfulness there that the very image that somebody has made as if it were a god can't even prevent itself from falling off a ledge.

Pagan rituals, in this author's judgment, pagan rituals turn into their own punishments. People who devout themselves to their passions stifle even the slightest inclination toward holiness and eternal life. Let me continue with the same passage:

> Afterward it was not enough for them to err about the knowledge of God,
> but they live in great strife due to ignorance, calling such great evils peace.

For whether they kill children in their initiations, or celebrate
  secret mysteries,
or hold frenzied revels with strange customs,
they no longer keep either their lives or their marriages pure,
but they either treacherously kill one another or ... [commit]
  adultery. ...
For the worship of idols not to be named
is the beginning and cause and end of every evil. ...
For it is not the power of the things by which men swear,
but the just penalty for those who sin,
that always pursues the transgression of the unrighteous.

I hear in that passage even some mocking satire about the fact that no
good Jew would ever speak the name, the sacred name of God in the
tetragrammaton. Here these idols should not be named. Our author
won't even go and name the idols that the Egyptians used or that
some of his contemporaries in Alexandria are using, not because
they're so sacred, but because they're so base.

We turn then to the next section; a section on death, incorruptibility,
and immortality. As in the opening section of this book, there are
several allusions here to immortality in the very final portion of this
book. Our author is entirely consistent in holding that immortality is
not simply a part of human nature, but God's gift. One sees some
ancient authors, I think of Plato for instance, trying to make an
argument that immortality is a natural part of human existence. One
can trace, for instance, four such arguments in Plato's dialogue, the
Phaedo. Rather, for our author, immortality is not a natural part that
we just have because it's part of us, but a gift that one must receive
from God, for God alone holds the power over life and death and it's
God's decision to give to the righteous this gift of immortality. One
sees this, for instance, at chapter 15, verse 3: "For to know thee is
complete righteousness, and to know thy power is the root of
immortality." Or one could look at chapter 16, verse 13: "For thou
has power over life and death; thou dost lead men down to the gates
of Hades and back again."

Interesting. The final portion, then, that we need to look at begins at
chapter 16 at the start and goes to the end of chapter 19, and this is
the rest of the plagues of Egypt. We already had the first one, but
now we're going to get, in relatively quick compass, all the rest of
the plagues. Each one of them is a punishment worthy of the crime. I

think of, for instance, Dante and his set of *contrapasso* in the section of the *Inferno* or the *Purgatorio*; there's something like that here. This final section of the text continues with the series of contrasts. It goes through each of the plagues but then it also takes the same element that's in one of the plagues and it uses the same element to talk about how God privileges and saves and prospers the righteous, those who have kept the commandments, even as it's using that very element to punish the ungodly who have violated the commandments.

This section is organized on the same model as that contrast that we saw between water and blood in chapter 11 but here, it's listing the ways in which God's divine wisdom is making use of some element of nature for the salvation of Israel and for the destruction of the Egyptians. Let me sort of talk through them rather than quoting much here. First, we get the frogs that showed up against Egypt. Well, by contrast we have quail for Israel. Then we get the locusts which were sent against Egypt and by contrast, Israel is experiencing a healing serpent in the desert. The third one, I'm up to chapter 16, verse 15 here, hail is sent against Egypt but of course, Israel receives manna. They find it on the ground and it feeds them each morning. Fourth one, darkness comes against Egypt but light comes for Israel; that's from chapter 17, verse 1 up to the beginning, verse 4 of chapter 18. The fifth one, very much more serious, death comes against Egypt but of course, there is rescue for Israel. We turn toward the end, by the time we get to chapter 19, to the Red Sea which is death for Egypt but of course, Israel is allowed to cross it. That same lesson is repeated in each of these contrasts. Let me just read one of them as an example of a text in which they bring out the lesson that we're supposed to learn. I'm reading from chapter 16, verse 24 but this gets repeated a number of times: "For the creation, serving thee who hast made it, exerts itself to punish the unrighteous, and in kindness relaxes on behalf of those who trust in thee."

The author draws the conclusion, it draws the moral for us right there. After this dramatically recounted set of comparisons using all the plagues, the book then ends on a note of very simple praise and I hear in this note of praise at the end, our author trying to summon those of his own people in Alexandria to join him in praise and to reflect on all this history and providence that he has been reviewing. It reads: "For in everything, O LORD, thou hast exalted and glorified thy people; and thou has not neglected to help them at all times and in all places."

As in Sirach, what is most prominent in wisdom literature of this sort is memory. Wisdom is a matter of keeping present to one's mind the covenant and the promises, mindful that God will fulfill these promises. The book as a whole, in this way, combines some of the most prominent approaches to wisdom that we have been seeing in the course of these lectures. In the cultivation of historical memory, the book functions like Proverbs and like Sirach to exhort us with the prospect of divine intervention on behalf of the just. But on the other hand, as we saw in the course of these lectures, there were also books like Job and Qoheleth that raised questions; so too here. And in general, these questions are about the time when evil seems to triumph. The answer comes in a way that it didn't come in Job and didn't come in Qoheleth. Here we get an answer; an answer that comes with immortality and even resurrection. God will vindicate the righteous in God's own time.

In the meanwhile, the counsel of the Wisdom of Solomon—while we're waiting for this divine intervention of providence to resolve the problem that for Job and for Qoheleth is unresolved—in the meanwhile, what the Wisdom of Solomon recommends is fidelity and prayer. So in the next lecture, I'm going to do what Solomon did and turn once again, this time, to another part of the Psalms to focus on the appropriate kind of prayer.

Lecture Thirty-Two
Interlude—A Wisdom Psalm on Torah

Scope:

Just as the latter books of biblical wisdom literature often emphasize the connections between Wisdom and Torah according to the traditional understanding of God's covenant with the chosen people, so too do a number of psalms. This lecture will focus on a psalm that exhibits this theme and then reflects on the importance of prayer for conforming oneself to the covenant that God has created. In the course of this lecture there will be an opportunity to reflect also on the theme of prayer for the spiritual gifts that are mentioned in Wisdom as well as in Isaiah.

Outline

I.   Praying with the Psalms.

    A. When we have paused for an interlude from the Psalms earlier in this course, a number of the specific psalms that we have used have involved moments of crisis, or at least intense feeling, but not all prayer is like that. In fact, much of the life of prayer, like much of life, is mundane (in its etymological sense of "day to day"), ordinary, and plain.

    B. Like the Psalter as a whole, the wisdom psalms cover a considerable range of possible situations, including angst, contrition, puzzlement, gratitude, and wonder.

II. Psalm 119 [118] on the love of God's law.

    A. In light of the close connections that we are seeing between biblical wisdom literature and the covenant, I would like to use this lecture for consideration of the psalm that is particularly devoted to the law, Psalm 119 [118].

    B. This is not only the longest of all the psalms (176 verses) but also the most formal in its structures. Each of its eight-verse sections corresponds to one of the letters of the alphabet, from aleph to tau.

    C. What we find in a psalm like this is a prayerful approach to living devoutly. It is a prayer praising God for providing such splendid laws for his people to live by.

D. Within each stanza, each of the eight verses begins with the same Hebrew letter. Most translations dare not even attempt to reproduce this structural feature.

III. Praying this psalm.

   A. In praying this psalm, it is highly appropriate to cultivate the same sort of humility that the psalmist has.

   B. In accord with one of the deep concerns of the sapiential tradition, the psalmist has a holy fear of the LORD—not a servile fear, but a mature one—wanting to honor his God and never disappoint him, but quite mindful of weakness.

   C. In public prayer with the Psalms, there is often a practice of having groups alternate the stanzas. This lets us speak some of the words and listen to some of the words. Mindful of the importance of local traditions in this matter, my only suggestion is that it can be helpful for everyone to grow used to a steady but relatively slow pace, and to allow for some moments of silence.

IV. Praying for wisdom.

   A. Repeatedly during the psalm, there are references to the quest for truth and insight. The more the psalmist ponders the Torah, the more he knows that God and his law are deeply true and yet how much more there is to understand.

   B. It is not simply a request for factual information. It is a request really to understand God's law, for God is good, and what God has done is good.

   C. C. S. Lewis notes how similar Psalm 19 [18] is to Psalm 119 [118] in this respect. After six verses about the orderly nature of God's cosmos and five about proper fear of the LORD and respect for God's law, the last four raise up a personal prayer.

V. Other suggestions in praying for wisdom.

   A. Within the prophets, there are many passages that pertain to wisdom. Let me mention just one from Isaiah that has had importance not only for Judaism but also within Christianity, which has a tradition of seeing in the prophecy about the Messiah contained in Isaiah 11:2 the biblical source for its doctrine of the gifts of the Holy Spirit.

B. Interestingly, the Septuagint translation of this passage uses "piety" (*eusebeia*) for the first of the two references to "fear of the LORD" in the Masoretic text, and this is the origin of the Christian notion that there are specifically seven such gifts.

C. One will find other references to a number of other gifts associated with the Spirit in various parts of the New Testament, including 1 Corinthians 12:8–10, Ephesians 4:11–12, and Romans 12:6–8.

D. In traditional Christian teaching, these gifts (usually listed as wisdom, understanding, counsel, knowledge, fortitude, piety, and fear of the LORD) are part of what Jesus Christ as the Messiah shares with those who become his adopted sisters and brothers sacramentally in baptism and confirmation.

E. One suggestion is to consider praying in the style of the psalms that we have been considering in this lecture, Psalms 119 [118] and 19 [18], for the gifts of the Spirit when we find ourselves in some special need.

VI. In the next lecture we will continue with the turn to Christian themes in the wisdom tradition by considering Jesus as wisdom teacher.

Suggested Reading:

Duggan, *The Consuming Fire*, 400–417.

Lewis, *Reflections on the Psalms*, chap. 6.

Mowinckel, *The Psalms in Israel's Worship*.

Questions to Consider:

1. What does it mean "to love the law"? How could one foster such devotion?

2. Psalm 119 [118] speaks both of God's justice and God's mercy. How do you understand divine justice and divine mercy?

3. What is meant by "the gifts of the Spirit"? What forms do they take in daily life?

Lecture Thirty-Two—Transcript
Interlude—A Wisdom Psalm on Torah

In this lecture we will turn once again to some of the wisdom psalms. Just as the latter books of biblical wisdom literature often emphasize a connection between Wisdom and Torah, according to that very traditional understanding of God's covenant with his Chosen People as being one of the great instances of wisdom, so too a number of psalms make that connection. This lecture will focus in particular on a psalm that exhibits this theme and then we'll reflect on the importance of prayer for conforming oneself to the covenant God has created. In the course of this lecture, there will also be an opportunity to reflect on the theme of prayer for the spiritual gifts that are mentioned in the Wisdom of Solomon as well being mentioned in Isaiah.

Let's turn first just to the question about praying with the Psalms in general. We've looked at that a number of times and I think we've had various insights. What I'd like to focus on in this lecture, in particular, is on the theme of regular prayer within one's life. I think that's something that both people who are in the household of the faith know about but also I think it's an object of concern for those who are still seeking or who are not of faith, that since this is such an important part of religious people's lives, it's important to understand why and how they make this such a practice.

In the past, in our lectures, when we paused for an interlude from the Psalms, a number of the Psalms that we have used have tended to focus on moments of special crisis, or at least they've been moments where there's been really intense feeling. But not all prayer is like that. In fact, much of the life of prayer, like much of life in general, is pretty mundane in the etymological sense of that word, of day to day, just ordinary and plain. In my experience, that prayer will be ordinary and plain is simply quite right and making a habit of prayer in the various ways one might pray; praise and adoration for example, or request and petition for what we need or those known to us need, sometimes very simply praying in gratitude and in thanksgiving for what God has already given. Or perhaps praying in sorrow and in contrition when we've noticed some faults, when we've noticed some failure. All of this is the normal stuff of a life of prayer. It needn't be anything of crisis. It can simply be the normal rhythms and the normal patterns of life.

Finding a place for each of these types of prayer will make it easier to come to God in those urgent moments of crisis. I have no doubt that God will hear us, even if we only come to him in a time of crisis. But whether we will think to come to God in a time of crisis or even if we think about it, whether we'll feel right about coming in a time of crisis when we haven't visited in a long time, well, frankly, it could be harder for us. And so part of what religious people do when they're trying to make a regular pattern out of a life of prayer even in the ordinary times, is simply having that familiarity with God so that when there are times of special need, they'll be calling upon someone who is, indeed, their friend and someone whom they trust and someone with whom they're used to speaking. I think that part of that is what's taking place in wisdom psalms, and I'd like to focus on that in this lecture.

Like the Psalter as a whole, the set of psalms that are called the wisdom psalms, they cover a fair range of possible situations. Some of the situations are those moments of angst, those moments of contrition. Those moments, like for Job, when it's puzzlement, those moments of gratitude and of wonder. In my judgment, the set of psalms that are often taken together as the penitential psalms speak to the heart in this concentrated way. This set is usually regarded, that is the set of penitential psalms, as numbering seven; namely, Psalm 6, and then Psalm 32. You remember that problem with the numbering, namely that if you're using the Hebrew text, it's one number higher. If you're using the Greek text, it's one number lower, so 32 or maybe in your Bible 31; 38 or 37, 51 or 50, 102 or 101, 130 or 129, and finally, 143 or 142. That's a set of psalms called the penitential psalms, a set that's very frequently used in the Christian churches. One finds them, for instance, in the season of Lent where they're said over and over again.

Although I do not know of any collective use of this set of seven penitential psalms in Jewish liturgy, each one of those psalms that I just mentioned has its own very distinct place within the course of the Jewish liturgical year. Psalm 51, for example, at least parts of it, are recited as an introduction to the *Amida* and they are the focal prayer in the *Siddur*. So it's a very important part of Jewish liturgical prayer too.

What I want to turn to though is not so much those, even though they have this great use as part of the ordinary life of prayer, I'd like to turn to Psalm 119—or 118 in some Bibles—Psalm 119, which is on love for God's Law. Let me begin by reflecting a little bit on the structure and the content and then we'll turn a little bit more to it's possible use and to some styles of prayer.

In light of the very close connections that we have just been seeing when we were reviewing the Wisdom of Solomon, those close connections between biblical wisdom literature and the covenant, I'd like to use this psalm, in particular, in the lecture we're doing now as an instance of how to pray in that regular pattern of prayer, particularly in light of the devotion to Law, to Torah, that we need.

Psalm 119 is the longest of all the psalms, it has 176 verses, but it's not only the longest, it's also the most formal in its structures. It consist of a series of stanzas and each stanza has eight verses within it but not just that it's eight per stanza, but rather, every line in the stanza begins with one of the letters of the alphabet. So there's a stanza in which all the opening words begin with aleph and then all of the opening words begin with bet; all the way through the entirety of the Hebrew alphabet.

This psalm makes no pretense to being an emotional outburst in the way that say, Psalm 51 does. Psalm 51 is often taken to be David's contrition after Nathan has just convicted him of adultery with Bathsheba and the murder of her husband Uriah, and this is David's emotional outpouring. Rather, Psalm 119 is a masterpiece of very elaborate and intricate pattern and it's a celebration of love for God's gift of the Law, God's gift of Torah. I talked earlier in our series about the book that C. S. Lewis wrote on the Law. Well, in the chapter within his book on the Psalms, C. S. Lewis discusses this psalm in particular, this psalm of love for the Law and he indicates in a very interesting way that presumably love for the Law doesn't mean that everyone will experience an exquisite feeling of delight or exhilaration at the specific commandments. It would be very interesting if what we felt was delight when we are hearing the commandment, thou shalt not kill or thou shalt not commit adultery or thou shalt not steal. Especially when we're tempted, usually love for those commandments isn't what we feel, but rather, when this psalm talks about love for the Law it does it mindful that we need to study and reflect and meditate on the Law and there are times within the meditations we'll have on the Law when we can see what a great gift it is.

This psalm, for instance, opens, verse 1, by saying "They are happy whose life is blameless, who follow God's law." It's very similar to the opening of Psalm 1, way back in the beginning of the Psalter because it focuses in on the delight. For instance, Psalm 1 in its first two verses talks about the delight that's involved in pondering Torah day and night. In this respect, the sentiment that's here is at least vaguely comparable to saying that you love your subject, you love history, or love philosophy, or love chemistry. A scholar loves the study of his subject and I think it's suggesting here, in the beginning of this psalm, that one can have a love for the Law and a love for studying the Law. The difference, of course, is that it is not just a natural delight in one's favorite subject but it's a really cultivated devotion that comes about when one has committed oneself to studying and really getting good at something that's just crucial. Here, a matter of what is crucial to living one's religion, a subject matter therefore that is very sacred. One dare not presume that theological learning alone makes one holy but perhaps by theological learning, by study, one will be moved to do the sort of the things that that study of the Law requires. In this way one is not guilty of some outrageous pride by suggesting that oh, by my study I became holy, but rather, by one's study of what is holy perhaps it will rub off; perhaps I'll start doing what it is that I study so hard.

Hence, what we find in a psalm like this, I think, is a very prayerful approach to living devoutly and letting one's study inform the structure of a devout life. It is a prayer praising God because God has provided such utterly splendid laws for his people to live by. The psalmist has right within the psalm an important component of expressing gratitude for the covenant that God has made with his people, and he's begging God for protection against those who get angry by fidelity to the Torah when it seems like just a burden. He acknowledges that there will be a great cost involved in obeying God's law. It's going to cut some of our desires, it's going to make us do things, but for the psalmist it's important to take that and to plead for wisdom, to understand more deeply and perhaps to be involved oneself in courting wisdom in the way we were talking about a little bit during our study of the Wisdom of Solomon when Solomon is busy courting Lady Wisdom, precisely that he will have this and that it will grow within him and that it will ultimately just fill him and fill his loves in his life. So too, the psalmist pleads for understanding this more deeply.

Within each stanza, each of the eight verses begins with the same Hebrew letter in any given stanza. Most translations will not even dare to attempt to reproduce that structural feature. You might want to check out the translation of the psalm that you like to use and see whether they even attempt this. But even if they are unable to find every appropriate word so that all the words will begin with "a" and all the words that will begin "b"; nonetheless, the structure that most translators find that they can easily incorporate so as to imitate the actual Hebrew text of this psalm, is to include within each stanza, one of the words that are taken up here as synonymous or at least as closely associated. So in many of the translations I've read, they'll find a way within each stanza to incorporate the following words: law, command, statute, decree, precept, word, saying, instruction, way. And by alternating within that set of words, what the translator will be doing is unifying the stanza because every stanza will have some group of those words and then the next stanza will repeat that same group of words. It's a way in which we can do it in English to try to capture the enormously sophisticated structure of this particular psalm.

Let me turn now to the question of praying with this psalm. So far I've just been talking about its basic literary structure and its content, but there's also the matter of thinking about how we might use it and how we might enter into the praying. In praying this psalm, it's highly appropriate, I think, to cultivate the same sort of humility that the psalmist has. It's not so much that the psalmist has already achieved perfection or that the psalmist is trying to LORD it over those who have not achieved perfection. If anything, the psalmist is mindful that he very much needs some help. So let me quote a little bit here that I think indicates some of that humility and that we might just want to dwell on for a little bit. I'd like to read verses 4 through 8 of that Psalm:

> You have laid down your precepts to be obeyed with care.
> May my footsteps be firm to obey your statutes.
> Then I shall not be put to shame as I heed your commands.
> I will thank you with an upright heart as I learn your decrees.
> I will obey your statutes: do not forsake me.

The accent here in those opening lines, I think, is on request, petition, asking God that he may, the psalmist, may hold firm, that he may learn more deeply what it is that God's law requires, not just what the words mean but what it is that the law is really asking. I think we all know how sometimes it can be ambiguous. What exactly is my obligation? What ought I to do? What does virtue demand? So

I think what he's asking is, is that he'll understand more deeply what the law requires and I think he's also very, very mindful that he needs God's grace to persevere. You know, I think for instance as I get older and was taking care of my aged parents, I was mindful of that commandment, thou shalt honor thy father and thy mother; but of course, what that commandment means when we're adults is different than when we're little tykes. For them, I suspect it means prompt obedience. Doing the dishes when we're told or cleaning up our room or stop fighting with our brother, but of course, as we get older adult what that fourth commandment might mean, well it's different. I think of even mom at the time when she had to be in the nursing home and she'd say, please take me home. Of course, I couldn't and part of what you have to do for her own good, is to honor her by keeping her in a safe place and then making sure to visit regularly and I have to admit I found it very interesting to reflect on what that fourth commandment meant at a very different time in my life. Well, I think part of what the psalmist is urging us to do, is to pray for that same grace, that same light of understanding, what it is that various commandments of God might actually require. One hears it also toward the end in verses 174–176 of the psalm:

> LORD, I long for your saving help, and your law is
> my delight.
> Give life to my soul that I may praise you. Let your
> decrees give me help.
> I am lost like a sheep; seek your servant for I remember
> your commands.

Even in that very curious image, you wouldn't expect at the end of this long psalm for him to say that he's lost like a sheep, and yet there's a way in which that might be the feeling that one bears and so he's still busily praying for light and for fidelity even at the end.

In accord with one of the deep concerns of the entire sapiential tradition, the psalmist also exhibits within this psalm, a holy fear of the LORD. We've talked about this before. It's not a servile fear, but it's a mature fear. It's a wanting to honor his God and never to disappoint him and yet, the psalmist, I think, is very mindful of his weakness. So in reflecting on a theme like fear of the LORD that's here, I think it's as much with a sensitivity to weakness as it is to anything that's sort of truly fearful in the strong sense of that word.

Okay, well with that in mind, how might we want to pray this psalm? How might somebody want to do it? Well, when praying by myself, I find that it can really help to bear in mind that piece of general advice that I mentioned in an earlier lecture; namely, there is no particular need to get to the end of the psalm, especially this one which has 176 verses. What makes more sense to me is, when I'm praying a psalm of this length, is to pause over verses that have some special bearing. I can remember a person that I very much trusted and who was a spiritual director of mine once, he used to say, "Stay with the fruit." What he meant by that little phrase is, if at a certain point along the course of praying this psalm, if some of the lines have a special resonance, if they make sense or if they perhaps move me to speak a little bit spontaneously on a subject, stay with the fruit. The rest of the psalm will be there. The text will remain for us and it'll be available for later in the time that I've allotted for prayer or the next time I come back to prayer and there's no particular need to get to the end of it. What there is needed, is if there is fruit because God is stirring something up and giving me, right then, some light for prayer or some particular feeling that I need to work out, stay with the fruit and abide there because that's perhaps where the real moment of prayer will come.

On the other hand, when I'm not praying it by myself but rather, with others, well one has to be sensitive to the fact that we are praying together. So in public prayer with the psalms that is used liturgically, whether in the various Christian churches or in the synagogue, there is a need to find some other way of praying. Frequently the practice is, at least in Christian churches, is to alternate the stanzas so that one part of the congregation will say this part and the other part will say the next stanza. This practice lets us speak some of the words and then listen to some of the words. So just as a few moments ago when I was urging that the translations may get all those different words for law and command and practice and precept, well, we'll say them and we'll have them in our minds precisely because we just voiced them and then when we're listening, that's part of what we'll hear is some of those very same words and terms being used but in a slightly different context. Mindful of the importance of difference in local traditions in this matter, some congregations say it differently than others do, my only suggestion is this; it can be really helpful for a congregation if people grow used to having sort of a steady but relatively slow pace. In fact, in some of the congregations I've been to, they're really comfortable with a little silence. So they don't jump in with the next stanza right after one is finished. It can help to have a little bit of a chance to let the words sink in.

There's also a matter of thinking about the fact that it's wisdom we're praying for. We were adverting to that when we were focusing in on the way in which Solomon was praying for wisdom. So too here, I think, with regard to something like Psalm 119. Repeatedly during this psalm there are references to the quest for truth and for insight. I get the impression when I'm reading through Psalm 119 of something here in the Bible that's spiritually akin to things that I know of in the philosophic tradition. I think, for instance, of the great hero of every philosopher, Socrates. At various points in his life, as recorded in the Dialogues of Plato, Socrates explained that there was once a Delphic Oracle that was about him and it made the striking statement that there is no one wiser than Socrates. And Socrates, confronted with that Delphic Oracle, had to give it an explanation. What he said was this, it was a very humble explanation. It wasn't that he knew or was wise because he knew so much but rather, that what he knew most of all was how much he didn't know and hence, he made it his practice very regularly, to stop in prayer, sometimes standing all night in prayer, and then to go in search of wisdom and to search for wisdom by asking the people that he knew, the people that he met, the people who were thought to be wise in the community. So he made it his practice to cultivate and to woo wisdom precisely by inquiring as well as by reflecting and praying.

Well, here in our psalm we see some of that, I think, in the biblical version of it. The more the psalmist ponders the Torah, the more he knows that God and his Law are deeply true, and yet how much more there is to understand than he might have initially envisioned. Let me give an example by quoting a couple of lines in that respect. These are lines that come from verses 65–68:

> LORD, you have been good to your servant according to
>   your word.
> Teach me discernment and knowledge, for I trust in
>   your commands.
> Before I was afflicted I went astray but now I keep
>   your word.
> You are good and your deeds are good; teach me
>   your statutes.

What I find in phrases like that is not simply a request for factual information. It is a request and here it is apparently a request made on the basis of some experience in the school of hard knocks. We don't get the exact context but he says that he had strayed and fallen away and hence what he's asking is the grace, the light, really to understand God's law. He can affirm God is good and that what God has done is good and he knows it both in the abstract and maybe by virtue of some experience that he's thinking of, but what he needs to do is to understand more deeply, not just to become convinced by some formal pattern of logic, but to accept and embrace and embody what God teaches us. When I think of other parts of the Bible where that's going on, you think of Leviticus, for instance, with its holiness code or you think of some of the ways in which, later on, Jesus is teaching in the Beatitudes, what our style and our approach to life is, or when he's reflecting on the commandments and doing so in light of Leviticus, he can say that thou shalt not kill means not only not to murder but not even to hold a sister or brother in contempt Or he can say, again in light of Leviticus, not thou shalt not commit adultery means not only not having sexual intercourse with someone who is not one's spouse but not even thinking lustful thoughts and fantasizing and getting all the other ways in which our minds can stray even internally even if our steps don't wonder. It's a matter of understanding it more deeply, what the commandment, what the Torah really requires.

In this way, Psalm 119 about love for the Law is a prayer for wisdom. Very close to the surface in the passages that I've quoted a few minutes ago, as well as many other parts of the psalm, very close to the surface is the same distinction that we have seen again and again recurrent in the wisdom books; namely, the distinction between the godly and the ungodly, between the virtuous and the vicious, between those who are righteous by keeping the law and those who are contemptuous of the law. The psalmist seems to me to be quite clear on the nature of this distinction, but he's also quite clear even though he hopes and he thinks he's on the right side, of begging for the strength to stay on the right side of that divide. To be with the sheep and not with the goats, precisely because our psalmist is mindful that it would be altogether too easy to go over onto the other side and if we're bright enough, it will be altogether too easy to provide some golden rationalizations because we can deceive ourselves very easily.

C. S. Lewis, in that same book that I've been discussing, C. S. Lewis notes how similar Psalm 19 is in this respect. Again, Psalm 19 in some Bibles, Psalm 18 in others. After six verses, about the orderly nature of God's cosmos and then five verses about proper fear of the LORD, he then turns to the question of respect for God's law and he makes that same kind of personal prayer in the last four verses, that prayer really to be faithful. This is Psalm 19 beginning around verse 12:

> So in them [he's referring to the decrees of the LORD] your servant finds instruction; great reward is in their keeping.
> But who can detect all his errors?
> From hidden faults acquit me.
> From presumption restrain your servant and let it not rule me.
> Then shall I be blameless, clean from grave sin.
> May the spoken word of my mouth, the thoughts of my heart,
> win favor in your sight, O LORD, my rescuer, my rock!

In that Psalm 19, I think one sees some of that same spirit and gets a sense of how to pray it. Let me close this lecture with just a couple of other suggestions about praying for wisdom. I turn in particular to the case of Isaiah and the gifts of the spirit. Within the prophets, there are many passages that pertain to wisdom but let me just, sort of concentrate for just a second on that one from Isaiah that has had such importance for Judaism and also for Christianity. Christianity has a tradition of seeing in the prophecy about the Messiah that is contained in chapter 11 of Isaiah, the biblical source for Christianity's doctrine of the gifts of the Holy Spirit. Let me begin by reading that:

> There shall come forth a shoot from the stump of Jesse,
> and a branch shall grow out of his roots.
> And the Spirit of the LORD shall rest upon him,
> the spirit of wisdom and understanding
> the spirit of counsel and might,
> the spirit of knowledge and fear of the LORD.
> And his delight shall be the fear of the LORD.

Interestingly, that translation is made, of course, from the Greek text but the Septuagint translation, that is the Hebrew translation into

Greek, the Septuagint translation of this passage uses piety, *eusebeia*, for the first of the two references to "fear of the LORD" that occur in the Masoretic text. So it's sort of equating fear of the LORD as the same thing as piety, one of those great gifts. This is the origin of the Christian notion, that there are specifically seven gifts not just six that are mentioned. One will find other references to a number of the gifts associated with the Spirit in various parts of the New Testament. You think, for instance, of I Corinthians 12; the fourth chapter of Ephesians; the twelfth chapter of Romans; in the fifth chapter of Galatians there's a list of the fruits of the Holy Spirit. In traditional Christian teaching, these gifts, which are usually listed according to the order of how they're found there in Isaiah: wisdom, understanding, counsel, knowledge, fortitude, piety and fear of the LORD, they're part of what Jesus Christ as the Messiah shares with those who become his adopted sisters and brothers sacramentally in baptism and confirmation. But taken more generally, these gifts are things that we can pray to be strengthened in any day and any time and any hour. They're important to pray for as part of this prayer for the gift of wisdom. So one suggestion that I have is this; namely, to consider praying in the style of the psalms in the ones that we've just been considering, Psalm 119 and Psalm 19, praying for the gifts of the spirit when we find ourselves in some special need. Perhaps it's praying for virtues like fortitude when we're afraid or praying for the gift of piety when we just kind of feel listless and not inclined to religious devotion, or praying for the various gifts associated quite directly with the gift of wisdom. For example, counsel both how to give good counsel and how to receive good counsel when it comes. Sometimes that can be the harder thing, taking good advice.

In the next lecture, we'll continue this trajectory here by turning to some of the Christian themes within the wisdom tradition and we'll be looking especially at Jesus as wisdom teacher.

Lecture Thirty-Three
Jesus as Wisdom Teacher

Scope:

We will focus here on Jesus of Nazareth as a wisdom teacher and as embodying divine wisdom. Christians understand him to be the second person of the Trinity, the divine Son of God the Father, and the Word of God. This lecture will present a brief overview of Christian teaching in this regard and will concentrate on the continuity between the way in which Jesus presents himself in the Gospels and the figure of the wisdom teacher that we have been studying throughout this course. We will also consider the focus of the Gospels on the death and resurrection of Jesus in relation to the treatment of death and resurrection in the book discussed in previous lectures, the Wisdom of Solomon.

Outline

I. Jesus as wisdom teacher.

   A. The Gospels show us the person of Jesus Christ—they recount his life story, his words and deeds (some of them miraculous), and his message, the proclamation of the kingdom of God.

   B. For the purposes of this course, I will concentrate on Jesus as the Wisdom of God and on Jesus as a teacher of divine wisdom. But it will be helpful to make some general points first.

   C. Christians believe that Jesus of Nazareth is the Son of God who took on our human nature for the sake of our salvation from sin and death. We understand God to be one in being or essence but also to be a trinity of persons: God the Father, God the Son (often called the Word of God), and God the Holy Spirit.

   D. It is Christians' belief that God so loved the world (John 3:16) that the Father sent his only Son to become one like us, and ultimately to suffer for us, to die, to rise, and thereby to redeem the human race and offer every person the invitation to salvation, to life eternal with God.

E. Even if a person does not have faith in the divinity of Christ, an open-minded hearing of his words may well lead to an appreciation for his wisdom.

F. As utterly innocent, he is thus the epitome of one who is unfairly made to suffer. He offers up that suffering and truly dies for us who are sinners. As the moment of that offering, Christians look to the incident at the very beginning of what is called his public life, around age 30, when he goes out to the River Jordan, where John, his cousin, is preaching that people should repent their sins and be baptized.

G. Christians understand by the symbolic action of John baptizing Jesus that the innocent and divine person of Jesus is at this moment taking upon himself all the sins of the world.

H. This moment is also understood to be the consecration of Jesus as the long promised Messiah, a Hebrew word that is translated into Greek as *christos* and into English as "Christ." It means "the anointed one"—the one anointed by God for a divine mission.

II. The place of the Gospels in the New Testament.

    A. The Greek term used to translate the Hebrew word for covenant (*berith*) is *diatheke*. In Latin, it is *testamentum*, which generates the words we use for the two parts of the Christian Bible, the Old Testament and the New Testament.

    B. At the heart of the New Testament are the four canonical Gospels: Matthew, Mark, Luke, and John.

    C. What is more relevant for us here is that the canonical Gospels seem to have been commissioned precisely to write down more accurate accounts of Jesus's life, as one can see, for instance, in the preface to the Gospel of Luke (1:1–4).

    D. In addition to the Gospels, the New Testament includes another historical book known as Acts of the Apostles that records the earliest days of the church, with special emphasis on Peter and Paul; and then various letters (Epistles) by Paul, James, Peter, John, and Jude; plus the letter to the Hebrews; and finally the book of Revelation (also known as Apocalypse).

E. As with the writings we considered from the Old Testament, there are various kinds of scholarly problems with the transmission of the Greek texts, with the identification of specific books as divinely inspired and appropriate for inclusion in the canon, and with translations. I will be using the Revised Standard Version.

III. Jesus and the wisdom tradition: continuity and novelty.

A. What one finds in the Gospels is an account of many things that Jesus did and many things that he said. The sayings take various forms: conversations, homilies, parables, short sayings (sometimes rather like the proverbs), and lengthy speeches.

B. There are a fair number of places where Christ himself comments about the connection between the old and new covenants, including an incident reported in all three of the Synoptic Gospels that uses the marital imagery that we noticed in the Song of Songs. He portrays himself as the long-awaited bridegroom who has now arrived.

C. In addition to stressing the continuity of the covenant relationship, Jesus also emphasizes that there is something new—that salvation comes now in his own person.

IV. Suffering, death, and resurrection.

A. Throughout our study of wisdom literature, we noted the tremendous problem of apparent injustice that is presented by the death of the young and the virtuous, the triumphs of the wicked during this life, and other comparable cases.

B. In such books as Daniel and the Wisdom of Solomon as well as in some of the psalms, divine revelation seems to be pointing toward the resolution of the problem in terms of life after death and God's eternal justice.

C. The suffering and death of Jesus is a preeminent example of unjust suffering of one who is innocent. But at the heart of the Christian story is the resurrection of Christ, which Christians understand as the conquest of death by the power of God.

D. The Christian understanding is that in addition to the judgment that individuals can expect after death, there will also be a last judgment at which the book of life will be opened and God will rectify all things.

V. With this introduction in mind, we will turn in the next lecture to the person of Jesus as teaching wisdom through his parables, and then in the following lecture to the Sermon on the Mount.

Suggested Reading:

The Apocryphal New Testament.

Benedict XVI, *Jesus of Nazareth.*

Neusner, *A Rabbi Talks with Jesus.*

Questions to Consider:

1. What does Jesus mean when he says that he came not to abolish the law but to fulfill it?

2. How is the biblical idea of "covenant" related to the idea of "testament"?

3. What is meant by the term "messiah"?

Lecture Thirty-Three—Transcript
Jesus as Wisdom Teacher

In the final portion of this course, we'll be turning to the subject of wisdom literature and the New Testament. Among the many important aspects of the life of Jesus of Nazareth at the very center of the New Testament, what I'd like to do in this lecture and the ones that follow is to focus on Jesus as a wisdom teacher, as well as embodying divine wisdom. As we'll see in the course of this lecture, Christians understand Jesus to be the second person of the blessed Trinity, the divine Son of God the Father, and the very Word of God. This lecture will present a brief overview of what Christian teaching is in this regard and will concentrate on the continuity between the way in which Jesus presents himself in the Gospels and the figure of the wisdom teacher that we have been studying throughout these course lectures so far, by looking at instances of wisdom books from the Old Testament. We will also consider, in this lecture, the way in which the Gospels focus on the death and the resurrection of Jesus and do that in relation to the theme and the treatment of death and resurrection in the book that we discussed just the previous couple of lectures, namely, the Wisdom of Solomon.

Let's turn then to start by considering Jesus as wisdom teacher; this is the element of continuity here. I'd like to divide it into two parts, namely to focus on the person of Jesus for awhile, again something probably well known to Christians, but to those who are still seeking, for those who are not as familiar with the presentation of Jesus in the Gospels, I'd like to focus a little bit on what Christians believe about that and then I'd like to talk about the genre in which we know it, namely the Gospels. The Gospels show us the person of Jesus Christ. They recount his life story over the course of 33 years. They give an awful lot of emphasis to the words that he said, sometimes individual sayings, sometimes much larger sermons or speeches, as well as the deeds that he did, whether it was recruiting the various disciples and training them or in some cases, miraculous deeds. So we'll need to take a look at what the Gospels show us in terms of his message, as well as his actions, and the message is especially a message of proclaiming the kingdom of God. Very frequently in the Gospels, one finds that phraseology used, namely that he announces that in his very person he brings the kingdom of God or sometimes the kingdom of heaven.

There are of course, many, many things that I would like to say about Jesus, far more than we have time to say in this series. And so I need to be highly selective here, but for the purposes of this course, what I will choose to concentrate on is Jesus as the wisdom of God and Jesus as a teacher of wisdom, a teacher of divine wisdom. In order to make that clear, I think it would be helpful to make a number of general points about what Christians believe first.

Christians believe that Jesus of Nazareth, that is, the individual who was the son of Mary, lived there at what we call the beginning of the 1st century, that Jesus is the son of God, someone who is from all eternity, a member of the divine Godhead, a member of the Trinity who took on our human nature for a purpose, namely for the salvation of the human race from sin and death. We, of course, have covered those topics frequently in the review that we've been making of biblical wisdom literature. In making these statements about Jesus, what Christians mean is that God exists eternally, not just through all time, but outside of time, independently of time. In fact, Augustine likes to say even time is one of God's creatures. Christians understand God to be One in Being, the technical word for that essence, but also to be a Trinity of persons; namely God the Father, God the Son, who is also called the Word of God very frequently, so God the Father, God the Son and God the Holy Spirit.

Admittedly, there is great mystery here, mystery that is simply beyond human comprehension, let alone beyond the scope of this course; how three can be one. My point is not to try to solve that problem here but simply to record some things about Christian belief that are relevant to our course and that might be helpful.

It is Christian belief that God so loved the world that the Father sent his only Son to become one like us. That's something recorded, for example, in a very short compass in the Gospel of John 3:16 and sometimes at football games or sporting events, one will see a sign held up John 3:16. What that particular passage is, is the testimony, God so loved the world that he sent his only son to become like us and ultimately to suffer for us, to die, but then to rise and in rising to do two things; to redeem the human race so that we ourselves would be freed from the burden of sin and secondly, to offer every single person the invitation to eternal life with God. The term Christians use to describe that is the term salvation, to offer to everyone the opportunity of salvation.

Even if a person does not have faith in the divinity of Christ, I think that an open-minded hearing of his words could well lead to a certain appreciation of his wisdom. One might think, for instance, of some of the great figures of the 20th century and the way in which, even though they were not believers in Jesus, nonetheless they had some of this understanding and attraction to his wisdom. I think of a figure like Gandhi in India and the veneration that he always showed for what he perceived to be the wisdom of Jesus. The list of those who have been inspired by Jesus in this way is endless.

What we will consider here in this lecture and the next two, is primarily the wisdom that he spoke in his words. But in light of our concern throughout this course, the concern that we've had with the problem of innocent suffering, there is also his deeds; the way in which he sometimes cured the sick, the way in which he healed those who were suffering severely, the way in which he brought some back from the dead, and then the deeds involving his own suffering, his own death, and his own rising. So it's not just his words that we need to look at but also these deeds.

According to Christian belief, then, Jesus is a divine person who took on a human nature from the moment of his incarnation—the technical word that means coming into the flesh—the moment of his incarnation in the womb of his mother, Mary. For Christians, Joseph is his foster father, not his biological father, for his true father is God the Father. In that way, by taking on flesh in the womb of the Virgin Mary, he had a human nature and a human nature that allowed him truly to be able to die and then to be raised from the dead. So Christians understand this to have been a real event, not just a pretense, not just somehow something that was feigned, but really dying after really suffering and then really being raised.

As someone who is utterly innocent, one who did not sin, one who is not guilty of anything, he is, in a way, the epitome of the one who is unfairly made to suffer. In fact, part of my reason for making sure to include that within the whole scope of our lecture series, is that we started with a figure who was also an innocent person who was unfairly made to suffer, the figure of Job. And what we saw early in the lecture series was that Job's story, the way in which as an innocent man he's made to suffer, it was kind of a test of his faith. Would he still be faithful in spite of having to suffer things that he did not deserve and having been accused by his friends of really having sinned and therefore, having suffered? So too, here at the end of the course, we look at someone who is the epitome of innocent suffering.

At the moment of that offering, namely that Jesus makes when he takes on our human nature and the time in which he fully accepts it, Christians look to a particular incident. It's described in the Gospels at the beginning of what is called Jesus's public life. He's initially conceived there of the blessed Virgin Mary and grows according to a normal pattern of life until about age 30. And at age 30 he undertakes his public life when he goes to the River Jordan, where his cousin, John, the one that we frequently call John the Baptist, is preaching very vigorously that people should repent their sins and be baptized. For John it's kind of a symbolic baptism. They have to go under the water and come up fresh from the water with the dirt or the sin washed off them.

Jesus also has that encounter. It's described in Matthew 3:13–17, for instance, and at that moment in the course of the Gospel of Matthew, when John the Baptist is baptizing Jesus, John the Baptist is suddenly given by God the grace to understand that the Jesus who has come to him, his cousin, the Jesus who has come to ask for baptism, is actually sinless; that there's no need for Jesus to undergo this baptism in the way that all the rest of the people in line need to undergo this baptism because of the history of their sinfulness. Even though he doesn't need to submit himself to the ritual of repentance because he has not sinned, he's doing it because he is taking upon himself the sinfulness of all the rest of humanity. At this point, John wants to say, mmm no you shouldn't be baptized, you don't need it. But Jesus, his cousin, insists, "Let it be so for now; for thus it is fitting for us to fulfill all righteousness." Those are the words of Jesus in Matthew 3:15.

By those words, Christians understand that Jesus is taking upon himself the sinfulness of all the rest of us. He says the words and he does this symbolic deed of receiving baptism at the hands of John, even though he is an innocent and in fact, a divine person, Jesus is at this moment fully accepting all the sins of the rest of the world. When he comes up out of the water after John has baptized him, according to the Gospels, the Holy Spirit, the third member of the Trinity, descends upon him in the form of a dove and then from heaven the Father says, "This is my beloved Son, with whom I am well pleased." One finds that not only in the text of Matthew, but in other ways one finds it early on in the Gospel of Mark, the Gospel of Luke, and the Gospel of John. This particular moment when the Father speaks, when the dove that is the representation of the Spirit is present, this moment is understood by Christians to be the consecration of Jesus as the long-promised Messiah. The Messiah, of course, that's a Hebrew word that is translated into Greek as Christos or in English as Christ; hence, Christ is not the last name of Jesus, rather it is a title and a title that means "the anointed one"; the one who has been anointed by God for a divine mission.

Now of course when Christians understand this to be the title that fits Jesus above all, it's actually placing Jesus in a long line, a long standing tradition of Judaism, of anointing certain people for the sake of the mission they have. Kings were anointed. They were anointed and regarded as God's anointed, so in a way the kings, David, or before him, Saul or after him Solomon, in a way they are messianic because they are ones who have been specially anointed by God for a mission. In this case, it's not just one in the series but for Christians, it is the culmination of the series, because this is someone who is the very Son of God who has received a human nature, has been living it through for 30 years, and now at this particular episode of the baptism in the River Jordan, he is now undertaking the mission and he receives this as his special anointing.

What is so decisive for Christians about this is that what Jesus then goes on to do in the course of the next three years that constitute his public life and the various things that he says, the things that make up the sayings of Jesus within the Gospel, as well as some of the sermons and speeches that he gives, all of these deeds and words are regarded by Christians not just as some good man's best efforts or some wise man's best thoughts. But rather, Christians understand them as the very wisdom of God which is now in human action and in human speech. In short, the teaching of Jesus is not just the product of human learning but rather, is something that makes very good and serious use of everything that had preceded in the revelation of God to Israel and is now in his own person coming direct and immediately from God the Father. That is a very strong claim but that's what it is that Christians believe about this.

Let me turn now from the person of Jesus, let me turn and try to give a brief introduction to the place of the Gospels within the Christian scriptures, within the New Testament. And by doing that, I think we'll also have ourselves rightly introduced for the third part of this lecture which will be a discussion about Jesus as wisdom teacher. From time to time in earlier lectures, I stressed the importance of the covenant as the sacred bond that God has made with Israel. In a way it's the most important theological idea of the whole Bible. It's a bond that God made with Israel and then every time it got broken, it was a bond that God renewed. So from Adam to Noah to Abraham to Moses to David, what Christians understand about Christ is directly understood in terms of covenant; namely what Christians think took place with the sacrifice of Christ is the fulfillment of a promise that had been recorded in the Old Testament, in particular, Jeremiah 31:31 speaks about the fact that there's going to come what's called a new and eternal covenant. Christians understand what Jesus's sacrifice to be, is the enactment of that new and eternal covenant. There's also a fairly long description of this in the letter to the Hebrews in chapter 8.

The Greek term that is used to translate the Hebrew word for covenant, *b'rith*—the Greek term is *diatheke*, and in Latin the translation of it is *testamentum*—that word, in turn, is the source of our word when we in English speak about Old Testament or New Testament. The Old Testament is called the Old Testament because it is in a way the history of the covenant that had been made and likewise, the New Testament is called the New Testament because it contains the record of the new covenant.

At the heart of the New Testament are the four canonical Gospels. Just as when we were discussing the Old Testament and the various parts of wisdom literature, what books were included on the list, and we regarded that as a canon or a rule for which books you read, so too, there is a New Testament canon and at the very beginning of it are those canonical Gospels: Matthew, Mark, Luke, and John. The shortest of them, Mark, is usually thought to have been written between the year A.D. 64 and 67. The others come after that but not too long after that, with John presumably coming from relatively late in the 1st century. John is the apostle thought to have lived the longest and he eventually writes the Gospel that bears his name last.

Three of the Gospels are called synoptic Gospels. It's a term that comes from Greek and it's related to the way in which one might have three different perspectives on the same episode, just as when there are, for instance, three witnesses to an auto accident or three witnesses to a crime. Well, Matthew, Mark, and Luke are the synoptic Gospels because their accounts follow the same basic story line very closely; the same basic stories, the same basic order with some variation, the same basic accounts of what Jesus said in either the same or at least closely similar words. There are admittedly some items that are only found in one of them or in another or perhaps in just two of them. On the other hand, the fourth of the Gospels, the Gospel of John, has a distinctly theological flavor and I use that word theological here in the sense that it contains even more reflection on the significance of what Jesus said and did that has already been recorded in Matthew, Mark, and Luke. In a way, it has longer continuous stories and they're done with even more artistry because they've had more time to work them out. And what one finds there is also very interesting from the wisdom literature point of view, that is, the specific project of our course.

In addition to those four Gospels there are other parts of the New Testament. There are going to be letters and there's eventually a book that's called Revelation, but when the church was putting together its canonical list, it did so precisely because it wanted to explain clearly what Jesus said and did. There are various scholarly issues here in regards to the dating of and the composition of these books. Most of those issues are beyond the scope of this course; fascinating, and I hope that sometime you'll have a chance to read or study that material.

I find it also very interesting to note that there were other attempts to write about the words and deeds of Jesus besides these four Gospels that are regarded as canonical. Some of them got a lot of publicity quite recently in things like *The DaVinci Code*. I think that that particular film and the book on which it's based seemed to be trying to suggest that somehow Church authorities were trying to cover up and to suppress something in those other earlier documents about Jesus. I don't think that's true.

In fact, these documents have long been in print and in my judgment, at least, you don't have to be a rocket scientist to understand why the Church came to see those particular accounts as inaccurate accounts of Jesus's life. In some passages, I think they border on the absurd. In the list of suggested readings for this lecture, I include some publication details, if you ever want to examine them. They are publicly accessible. What's much more relevant for us, here in this course, are the four canonical Gospels. And it's important to know that those four canonical Gospels, Matthew, Mark, Luke, and John, they were commissioned precisely so as to write down more accurately, good accounts of Jesus's life, Jesus's deeds and Jesus's words. You might want to look sometime at the preface of the Gospel of Luke, the first four verses of the first chapter, because there he even reports how carefully he's trying to do this. He needs to correct what some of the false versions were.

In addition to those four Gospels, the New Testament, as I said, includes a historical book known as the Acts of the Apostles and what that does is to record the earliest days of the Church with special emphasis upon Peter and Paul. And then there are various letters usually known as Epistles. There are a fair number by Paul, James, Peter, John, and Jude and then there's one called the letter to the Hebrews, so it's a letter in a way to the Jewish community. And finally, the book of Revelation, sometimes known as the Apocalypse. There is much wonderful and fascinating material here. I will only discuss just a very brief bit of it in so far as it's directly relevant to the theme of wisdom.

As with the writings that we were considering from the Old Testament, there are many kinds of scholarly problems. There are, for instance, the problems of the transmission of the Greek text, just as there were transmission problems with the transmission of the Hebrew text. There are problems with the identification of which books are by which person and which books are divinely inspired, which books were chosen for inclusion in the canon. And then, of course, there is the great problem of translations. It is very interesting to know that the earliest complete Greek text of the whole New Testament that still exists comes from the 4th century A.D. and that scholars have been able to resolve a tremendous number of textual variations by the very careful application of their methods. Just as when we were reading from the books of the Old Testament, I would invite you to consider how the translation that you might have on hand or that you might prefer, how it renders the Greek text into English. For the most part I will be using the Revised Standard Version, the RSV translation, but you might want to consult some of the other translations. I'm a great fan, for example, of the Navarre Bible which includes the Latin Vulgate translation as well as the RSV and a little commentary on each page.

2009 The Teaching Company.

Let me turn now to the other part that we need to have in this opening lecture from the New Testament, namely a focus on Jesus and the wisdom tradition. What I want to emphasize here in this part is the continuity of Jesus with the biblical wisdom tradition that we've already been considering; the continuity but also the novelty, the elements that are genuinely fresh and new and original.

Bringing from one's own storehouse the old and the new, that's one of those proverbs that's attributed to Jesus and in a way it's an accurate title for what we need to be doing here in the remainder of this lecture. What one finds in the Gospels is an account of many things that Jesus did and many things that Jesus said. The sayings of Jesus take various forms. Some of them are the give and take of conversation; some of them are clearly homilies. There are also parables and we'll spend a whole lecture dealing with his parables. Sometimes there are very short sayings that are rather like the Proverbs and there are relatively lengthy speeches. At the conclusion of one of the sets of parables—we'll consider more of the details of that in the next lecture—Jesus himself comments on the theme of continuity and of novelty. I'd like to read that passage to set the stage here. This is chapter 13, verse 52 of Matthew: "Every scribe who has been trained for the kingdom of heaven is like a householder who brings out of his treasure what is new and what is old."

There's a sense right there in Jesus's own words about continuity and novelty. There are, of course, a fair number of places where Christ himself comments about the connection between what we call the Old Testament and the New Testament, that is, between the old covenants in all of their history and this new covenant which he is introducing. There is within that set of places where Jesus describes this, there's an incident that is reported in all three of the synoptic Gospels that I think is also very helpful and I'd like to read it here. It uses the marital imagery that we were noticing in the Song of Songs and before that, in some of the Prophets. Jesus portrays himself as the long awaited Bridegroom who has now arrived. This is taking from the translation of Mark 2:

> Now John's disciples and the Pharisees were fasting; and people came and said to him, "Why do John's disciples and the disciples of the Pharisees fast, but your disciples do not fast?" And Jesus said to them, "Can the wedding guests fast while the bridegroom is with them? As long as they have the

bridegroom with them, they cannot fast. The days will come, when the bridegroom is taken away from them, and then they will fast on that day. No one sews a piece of unshrunk cloth on an old garment; if he does, the patch tears away from it, the new from the old, and a worse tear is made. And no one puts new wine into old wineskins; if he does, the wine will burst the skins, and the wine is lost, and so are the skins; but new wine is for fresh skins."

Words like these from Jesus are, I think, part of the basis for understanding that God has presented himself in Jesus as a husband to Israel; that is, it's an image which Jesus is clearly using in that particular passage, likewise Paul in some of his letters will develop this and subsequent Christian theology will frequently make use of it. The notion that Christ is a husband for Israel, that he is, in a way now, betrothed to this new Church which he is founding, so too, just as God was a husband to Israel, Christ is a husband for the new Israel that is the Church. One might have a look at the second chapter of Ephesians for that. In addition to stressing the continuity of this covenant marital relationship, Jesus is also emphasizing that there is something really new here; namely that salvation has now come in his own person.

There's a similar point in the way in which Jesus comments on the Law. I'd like to read a short passage here. This time from Matthew 5:

Think not that I have come to abolish the law and the prophets; I have come not to abolish them but to fulfill them. For truly, I say to you, till heaven and earth pass away, not an iota, not a dot, will pass from the law until all is accomplished.

One sees there even in his own words a sense of two of the three major parts of the Bible that he knew; namely the Law and the prophets. His suggestion is he has come not to abolish them, but to fulfill them. He has come, I think, to bring them to a fulfillment and to deliver a wisdom within his own person.

Let me also comment for just a minute on that great question that we have been asking ourselves about from the beginning of this course; namely the problem of the suffering of the innocent. In addition to many other passages that could be quoted from what Jesus said, I would also like to emphasize here the continuity and the novelty between Jesus and the wisdom tradition on the problem of evil, of suffering, of death, precisely because the Gospels culminate not just with the death of Jesus but with his resurrection. Throughout our study of wisdom literature, we noted the tremendous problem of the apparent injustice that doesn't seem to get corrected in this life, a problem that is presented by the death of the young, the death of the virtuous, the triumphs of the wicked during life, and other comparable cases that we kept studying. But in such books as Daniel and the Wisdom of Solomon, as well as in some of the Psalms, it seems to me that divine revelation kept on pointing toward the resolution of the problem as a resolution that really has to take place after this life, after our death. It has to get resolved by God's eternal justice. The suffering and death of Jesus, combined with his resurrection, is an answer to that problem. The suffering and death of Jesus is a pre-eminent example of unjust suffering on the part of one who is innocent. But at the heart of the Christian story is the resurrection of Christ which Christians understand as the conquest of death by the power of God. For instance, understanding Genesis 2:17 to say that death enters the world precisely because of sin, Paul notes in his letter to the Romans, chapter 6, "For the wages of sin is death, but the free gift of God is eternal life in Christ Jesus our LORD."

The Christian understanding of a passage like that, in addition to the judgment that individuals can expect after death, is that there will also be a general or last judgment. Some of that's described in the book of Revelation at chapter 20, at which time the book of life will be opened and God will rectify all injustice.

Well, with this introduction in mind, in the next lecture we will turn to the person of Jesus, precisely as teaching wisdom through his parables. And then in the following lecture, I'd like to take as an example of Jesus the wisdom teacher, one of his sermons, the Sermon on the Mount.

Lecture Thirty-Four
Jesus and the Wisdom Stories in the Gospels

Scope:

One of the recurrent features of the life of Jesus recounted in the Gospels is his frequent habit of telling wisdom stories in the form of parables. This lecture will give a general orientation to the structure of the four Gospels and then focus on the parables. After offering some reflections on the nature of parables as a genre of wisdom story, this lecture will propose a classification of the various parables found in the Gospels, along with more detailed study of some representative samples, including the parable of the sower and the seed, the parable of the good Samaritan, and the parable of the prodigal son.

Outline

I.   The parable as a wisdom story.

    A. As we have seen throughout our survey of biblical wisdom literature, there are various genres that have proven useful: proverbs, drama, extended conversations, history. One of those most typical for Jesus is the parable. The Gospels contain more than 40 parables.

    B. A parable is a brief story to illustrate some teaching or lesson. Although the use of the parable (in Hebrew, *mashal*) is relatively limited in the Old Testament, many such parables are found in the Talmud and in the Midrash.

    C. While the category of *mashal* encompasses a wide variety of genres besides the parable, the parable (taken more narrowly) tends to be a quite simple illustration by way of comparison.

    D. There have been periods in the history of scriptural interpretation that regarded all parables as allegorical. There certainly are passages that put an allegorical interpretation of a given parable on the lips of Jesus, but I would caution against any insistence that this is always the case.

    E. There are various ways of classifying the parables of Jesus. One way to do this makes use of the chief function of each kind.

II. Jesus's use of parables.

   A. In all three of the synoptic Gospels, we find the answer that Jesus gave to the question about why he preached in parables. It is admittedly mysterious.

   B. The better interpretation, I think, depends on reading them in light of the passage that he cites here from the prophet Isaiah and from his own life. It is a passage in which the prophet Isaiah laments his failure—not surprising, for prophets inveigh against prevailing opinions in which people are very comfortable.

   C. Presumably it is for precisely this reason that the comment on why he preaches in parables comes here, just before his allegorical explanation of the parable of the sower, in which those sowing the seed are preaching the kingdom of God.

   D. What the parable form often does is allow the expression of wisdom through paradoxes—those apparent contradictions that require us to think through the words and the story to a deeper point than the story at first seems to express, and one that our rationalism might have disinclined us to accept.

III. Let's consider some other parables of Jesus that are rightly famous for being distillations of the distinctive wisdom that is his, the parables of the good Samaritan (Luke 10:25–37) and the prodigal son (Luke 15:11–32).

   A. When a scholar of the law tries to test Jesus by asking him what he needs to do to gain eternal life, he already knows what the Bible has to say. Jesus turns the question back on the scholar, who then combines the directive from Deuteronomy 6:5 with that of Leviticus 19:8 in a formulation that Jesus heartily approves.

   B. What elicits from Jesus the parable is the follow-up question on how this is to be applied in practical life by consideration about just who this "neighbor" is: another member of one's own community? Or does it also include the foreigner?

   C. The mercy that the parable has the Samaritan show leads to the quite unexpected conclusion that the needs of another require that I must become a neighbor, whether I feel like it or not, in order to observe the law.

D. What provokes the parable of the prodigal son, his unforgiving brother, and the father who would try to reconcile them is the way in which some Pharisees and scribes were "murmuring" against Jesus's practice of eating with tax collectors and other sinners.

E. According to the story, the younger brother gets his father to advance him his share of the inheritance and runs off to squander it on a life of wine, women, and song.

F. Within his conscience, the young man realizes that he needs to repent his offense against his father and hope for at least a position in his father's household where he can work like a hired hand. His father kisses him and embraces him and has the fatted calf killed for a feast to welcome the prodigal son back.

IV. The text of Luke moves on to other parables: the dishonest steward (16:1–13) and the case of Lazarus and Dives (16:19–31), both of which also bear on the situation then before Jesus in the persons of the Pharisees and the tax collectors.

A. From our viewpoint in considering Jesus's use of parables for his distinctive wisdom teaching, the point is presumably clear: There is need for justice and for mercy. Not only are they not opposed, they are both necessary. There is no excuse for injustice, and the rupture of social relations involved in sin must be restored.

B. The parables, in my judgment, are fundamental to the divine perspective of Christ's wisdom. They present the message in unforgettable ways. In the next lecture we will turn to one of Jesus's most famous sermons, the Sermon on the Mount, to see him teaching his wisdom in the form of a lengthy discourse.

Suggested Reading:

Benedict XVI, *Jesus of Nazareth*, chap. 7.

Dodd, *The Parables of the Kingdom*.

Jeremias, *The Parables of Jesus*.

Questions to Consider:

1. Why does Jesus use parables for the communication of his message?

2. "Love your neighbor as yourself." How do you understand "neighbor"? What obligation is there here? If there are limits to that obligation, what are they?

3. In the story of the prodigal son, does the older brother have any right to complain to his father of injustice?

Lecture Thirty-Four—Transcript
Jesus and the Wisdom Stories in the Gospels

One of the recurrent features of the life of Jesus as it is recounted in the Gospels is his frequent habit of telling wisdom stories in the form of parables. This lecture will give a general orientation to the structure of those four Gospels that we were talking about in the last lectures and then we'll focus in on the parables. After offering some reflections on the very nature of parables as a genre of wisdom story, this lecture will go on to propose a classification of the various parables that are found in the Gospels, along with more detailed study of some representative samples. I'll focus a little bit on the parable of the sower and the seed and then at greater length on the story of the good Samaritan and the story about the prodigal son.

Let's begin with just thinking about parable as wisdom story because this is something throughout the Bible that has a great importance; the very genre of parable. As we have seen throughout our study of biblical wisdom literature, Old Testament and New, there are various genres that have proven useful for us to know about; Proverbs with which we started, those short maxims; drama where wisdom comes by the interplay of characters; extended conversations as in the Song of Songs or history as we saw it, for instance, in the book of Sirach. One of these most typical genres with regard to Jesus and the way in which he speaks is the parable. The Gospels contain more than 40 parables.

A parable is a brief story that is used to illustrate some teaching or lesson. Although the use of the parable is relatively limited in the Old Testament, it is found, the word for it is *mashal*. It's a parable; it can also mean a riddle. It's relatively limited but there are, on the other hand, many parables found in the Talmud and a tremendous number of them in the Midrash. One of the most famous parables is the one that Nathan tells David. For this one, we'd look at the second book of Samuel, the twelfth chapter. The prophet Nathan confronts David and he tells him a story about a very wealthy man who took the single lamb that had been raised by some poor neighbor, to provide a meal for a guest. David immediately grows incensed. He thinks that that man has done a wicked thing but then, right after that he feels utterly convicted, for the prophet Nathan tells him, you are that man. And David realizes that the adultery that's he committed with Bathsheba and then the murder of her husband, Uriah, is in fact indicated by this parable. The prophet Nathan kind of had him fooled; he had him going. He was so into the story and then he realizes that it applies to himself.

While the category of *mashal* encompasses a wide variety of things besides parables in the strict sense, there are things like allegories; there are fables, proverbs, riddles, symbols, examples, sometimes even jokes and jests. If you take the genre parable a little bit more narrowly, it tends to be a matter of simple illustration, usually by way of a comparison. And the clarity of the comparison adds to the forcefulness of the parable and yet the depth that can occur in even a short and direct and simple comparison, it means that we should again and again and again ask what exactly is it that Jesus wants us to grasp in the parables that he tells. Sometimes it's pristinely clear. Sometimes what we're left with is a question. Yes, there's a comparison, what is it that he most wants us to know?

There had been periods in the history of the interpretation of scriptures that tried to say all parables are allegorical; that is, they all have a whole separate level. Now there certainly are passages that use an allegorical interpretation of a parable and even put the interpretation on the lips of Jesus; one example of that is found in the Gospel of Mark 4: 1–20, and it's the parable of the sower. The sower goes out to sow the seed. Well, after Jesus has given the parable, then he steps back and he gives his own allegorical interpretation of each point in detail, about that parable. There are such parables, but I would caution against using any insistence here that this is always the case; namely, that every parable is allegorical, at least in the way of those particular scriptural interpreters who found the text of the parable no longer acceptable as they stand and they were looking for some other more remote interpretation, perhaps some philosophical opinion that was hidden behind the literal or plain meaning. For example, there are some theorists who don't like the fact that Jesus was intending to found a Church or that Jesus was really looking ahead to heaven and instead, they treat his parables that are parables about the kingdom of heaven as if all of them pertained to what is called in the technical literature, an imminent eschatology; that is, a proclamation of the kingdom of God that belongs exclusively to this world, as though Jesus's message were limited to some pattern for a new social order or some program for a new political order. I think that that kind of interpretation does violence to the texts and I suspect that that strategy, frankly, I suspect that that strategy reveals more about the interpreter than about the text. We should be a little bit more open-minded than that and simply take it as a question. What is it that the parable is intended to suggest to us?

The types of parables are several and we do well to ponder that question of classification of parables. There are various ways of organizing a classification for the parables that Jesus tells. One way to do it that I particularly prefer and would like to recommend to you, is this, a classification that's based on the main function that the parable has and there are a couple that are listed. I'll propose them and perhaps you might want to make it a project in your own reading of the Gospels. What classification would you use? How would you organize them?

One function that some of them have is the function of likeness; that is, whether it's a simple simile, x is like y, or something slightly more extensive, even though it doesn't have full development like a narrative would have. There's often something about the likeness in a parable. For example, at the Gospel of Mark in chapter 40 at verse 32, it reads, "The Kingdom of God is like a grain of mustard seed" and I think what we're supposed to do is to say, well okay how is it like a mustard seed? And in the text it goes on to talk about the fact that mustard seeds are tiny but they grow into enormous bushes and the suggestion is the kingdom of God starts small but grows very large. It's all in that one element of a likeness. There are lots of points of difference, but when one grasps the simple point of likeness, one gets the parable. Here's another one; it comes from Matthew 13:33, "The Kingdom of God is like yeast that a woman took and mixed in with three measures of flower." Well similarly, that particular parable is a very simple likeness, a very simple comparison and it's good at one level for suggesting that a tiny little bit of yeast will make all the flour rise and will make the bread rise. The other points are points of difference and there's no particular comparison, but when one gets that direct likeness, one has some of the parables figured out.

A second use, stories; stories that have a narrative with a little bit of plot development. Those comparisons between the kingdom of God and the yeast or the kingdom of God and the mustard seed don't have any plot development, but some of the parables tell a story. In fact, they might even give a conflict that needs to be resolved. For example, there's the parable of the vineyard and the plot development occurs over the problem of how to pay the workers; namely, they've all done the same job of working but they've done it for very different amounts of time. How should they be paid? We might expect that they'd be paid different amounts because of the different amount of time that they worked, but the surprise in the parable is that they all get paid the same wage at the end of the day. Many people have seen this as a parable about the fact that whether you're baptized as a child and grow up as a Christian, or whether you only come to the faith much later on, still the reward is the same of eternal life with God in heaven. Later on in this lecture, we'll consider a little bit about another one of those problem parables, one that focuses on a story with a plot; namely the parable of the prodigal son that's in Luke 15.

Let me go on to a third possible function as a way of classifying parables. It might be that the parable is designed to give an example. These are the parables which have a story and a plot but the plot doesn't so much come to provoke a problem, to make us think, but rather, the plot is designed to exemplify some conduct that is clearly being recommended or some conduct that is being discouraged. For example, there's the story of the good Samaritan that's told in Luke 10, beginning at verse 25 where clearly what we're supposed to do is think about imitating the good Samaritan. Likewise, there's a famous parable, the story of the Pharisee and the tax collector who are praying in the Temple, and the Pharisee is up front, really making a big production of it and explaining to God all the wonderful things he's done, where in the very back of the Temple is the tax collector praying very simply and the question is, is which of these is the right kind of prayer? So I would propose that likeness, that the great plot development for the sake of problem or the exemplification, are some of the classifications that can be used and by having a classification system, one can think about the various ways and the purposes that these parables are supposed to serve.

Let's turn now to Jesus's use of parables, because over 40 times in the Gospels he does this. It's not just something that we can get by looking at all the various examples. That's one good way of doing it, but he even tells us something about his reason for preaching in parables. As it turns out, in all three of the synoptic Gospels, we find the answer that Jesus gives to the question about why he preaches to the crowds in parables. Admittedly, his answer is a bit mysterious and it'll take us a few minutes to talk our way through this. Let me read it in the passage that comes in the Gospel of Mark. I think it's absolutely fascinating how he does this. This is Mark 4:

> And when he was alone, those who were about him with the twelve asked him concerning the parables. And he said to them, "To you has been given the secret of the kingdom of God, but for those outside everything is in parables; so that they may indeed see but not perceive, and may indeed hear but not understand; lest they should turn again, and be forgiven.

Now, that's a very curious answer, isn't it? You talk in parables so that they don't get it? Hmm, we need to think about that. What immediately follows in this text is then the allegorical interpretation of the parable of the sower; that is, he's described the image of the sower and then himself gives to the apostles who are seated around, the interpretation of what he wants that parable to mean. Here I just wanted to cite his general comments about the use of parables, because it sounds in the text that I just read, it sounds as if Jesus were taking a very gnostic line, trying to make a secret out of this, trying to make his message inaccessible, except to those very few who have been initiated. I don't think that's what's up.

A better interpretation, I think, depends on reading the words that I just said, in light of the passage that Jesus here himself is citing from the prophet Isaiah and then comparing the passage he cites and his own life. Let me read from the full text from Isaiah. To my mind, it's really got to be done this way and it's interesting that in Christian churches, liturgically, usually this passage from Isaiah is read on the same Sunday that we read that mystifying explanation of the parables. I think it's going to make it all make sense. This is from Isaiah 6:10:

> Make the heart of this people fat, and their ears heavy, and shut their eyes;
> lest they see with their eyes, and hear with their ears, and understand with their hearts, and turn and be healed.

Now, those words are from Isaiah; Jesus is quoting them in the explanation that he gives. It's a passage in which the prophet Isaiah is lamenting his failures, not surprisingly of course, for prophets constantly were inveighing against the prevailing opinions in which the people to whom they were commissioned to speak are very comfortable and don't feel as though they really need the LORD. The prophet Isaiah is commissioned to speak and to tell them your comfort is really an illusion and you need to turn in faith because the LORD is just about to send a great challenge and only he will be able to resolve it.

Well, looking ahead to the rest of the life of Jesus, he too confronts the prospect of utter failure, not being understood and eventually dying on that cross. The cross will be the source, as it turns out, of great fruitfulness but it sure looks like the end. It sure looks like defeat. It sure looks like failure. It is, for a Christian understanding, only through the suffering and death of Christ the victim, that the resolution of the problem of evil takes place. Parables like these, speak in a hidden way but a way that can be revealed, they speak of the mystery of the cross. They speak of the need for suffering in the life of Jesus as what he intends. It's not something that hits him, that he didn't know was coming, but is in fact his very intention in coming in this life. As with Isaiah, the life of Jesus will appear to end in failure but only in that apparent failure will the full meaning of the sacrifice become clear; namely, the eyes and the ears of onlookers will be opened and the mercy of God will, in fact, bring healing. Jesus understands his sacrifice as the sacrifice that comes with the new and eternal covenant. He has to be sacrificed for it to be enacted.

Presumably, it is for precisely this reason that the comment on the reason for his preaching in parables takes place and uses this passage from Isaiah, just before his allegorical explanation of the parable of the sower. In that allegorical explanation that he gives of the parable and the sower, those sowing the seed, he says, are preaching the kingdom of God. As every culture that has ever been tempted by famine to eat its seed rather than saving it as seed corn, the culture will be tempted because of the famine to eat that seed corn; casting the seed on the ground seems to miss the need of taking care of current needs. In fact, as any culture knows, you've got to use the seed corn and plant it. You can't eat the seed corn or else you're going to miss the real resolution of the problem.

Well, Jesus returns to this very image of seed and the need of seed to die. He returns to this image at the final leg of his journey in Jerusalem, the thing that Christians commemorate on Palm Sunday. Let me read that and I think it'll bring this whole mystery of how to interpret his use of parables together. This from the twelfth chapter of John:

> The hour has come for the Son of man to be glorified. Truly, truly, I say to you, unless a grain of wheat falls into the earth and dies, it remains alone; but if it dies, it bears much fruit. He who loves his life loses it, and he who hates his life in this world will keep it for eternal life. If anyone serves me, he must follow me; and where I am, there shall my servant be also; if any one serves me, the Father will honor him.

This passage, I think, is the kernel and if you'll excuse the pun, the kernel of the wisdom of Jesus, the admittedly counterintuitive message that to live, one must die; that to receive the matchless treasure of eternal life, one must be ready to lay down this earthly life; that to be rightly ordered in one's loves, one must be generous rather than acquisitive.

As in so much of the wisdom literature that we have already been studying, the point is not the communication of some abstract knowledge, but rather it is a matter of getting someone who sees but doesn't quite perceive or understand what he's seeing, someone who hears but doesn't really grasp, moving such a person to the mystery of God, toward the needing to die in order to live, of Christ needing to sacrifice himself in order to make this redemption and thus eventually to grasp something that matters very deeply for personal life; namely, a change of life. It's not just some addition to our stock of knowledge but it's going to be a wholesale and complete change, a conversion of heart, what in Greek is called *metanoiein*.

What the parable form that Jesus is discussing here in his explanation of why he teaches in parables, what the parable form often does, is to allow the expression through paradoxes. A paradox, of course, is an apparent contradiction and the parable form allows the expression of wisdom through a paradox that requires us to think through the words and to think through the story to a deeper point that the story really is trying to convey but a far deeper point than it seems to express, one that our rationalism might've made us disinclined to accept. It's the reason I think why some of those interpreters, they can see what the point is and they don't like it and hence, they try to give it a different understanding that pertains more to a worldly or secular understanding.

Let's turn now and use this understanding of why Jesus teaches in parables and let's use it to consider some of the parables that he teaches, beginning with the parable of the good Samaritan. By looking at this, what we'll see is that they are really distillations of the very distinctive wisdom that is Jesus's own. I'll also, before we're through, look at the parable of the prodigal son. But here in this first one, the parable of the good Samaritan that comes from Luke chapter 10, beginning at verse 25 and going on to verse 37, it starts with a scholar of the Law; someone who is very deeply knowledgeable about Torah and he's trying to test Jesus. He asks him what he needs to do to gain eternal life. He explains he already knows what the Bible has to say on that subject. Jesus turns the question right back on the scholar and in the course of it, in the course of turning it back on the scholar, he combines two passages from Torah in a formulation that Jesus hardly approves; namely, from Deuteronomy 6:5 and from Leviticus 19:8. Here's the passage and it describes what Jesus regards as the right answer: "You shall love the LORD your God with all your heart, and with all your soul, and with all your strength, and with all your mind; and your neighbor as yourself."

Jesus approves the answer the scholar gives. It elicits from Jesus a parable. It's sort of a follow-up question that has to be asked, well how do I do this? How do I know, in fact, who is my neighbor? Is this just somebody from my own community? Is it some relative? Is it the guy who lives next to me? Does neighbor also include the foreigner? Well, when the scholar asks, who is my neighbor, it elicits from Jesus this parable of the good Samaritan. In the parable, a priest and Levite pass by someone who has been robbed and beaten and left dying on the roadside, but then a Samaritan who happens by has pity and takes the victim to an inn for care, despite the fact that this man would not have been a neighbor in the sense of a member of the victim's community. By having a Samaritan do it, we have somebody who is not a neighbor but somebody who would've been regarded as from a whole different sect, with whom we don't like to have any dealings. What this does, is to expand the very restricted sense of who "neighbor" is.

The mercy that the parable shows the Samaritan giving leads to the quite unexpected conclusion that the needs of another require that I must somehow become the neighbor of a person in need whether I feel like it or not. Even if I have pressing business like the priest and the Levite presumably had, maybe I have to be doing something to try to observe the Law but if I see somebody in need, in particular dire need, and no one else to help, there is need for me to be neighbor to such a person. Considered then as a wisdom teaching, as a teaching in this tradition of wisdom literature we've been studying, the parable is profoundly like the point that so much of the rest of the Bible has been making. a deep reverence for the Law expressed through a profound and presumably unexpected application. I think you see both the continuity and the novelty; deep reverence for the Law, but something genuinely new by determining for us who is the neighbor, perhaps someone very unexpected.

Let's take a second example, namely the parable of the prodigal son, because I think that this too shows us both the continuity and the novelty of Jesus's teaching. He's in the tradition but he has a very distinctive take and it comes from his own, I think, divine source. What provokes the parable of the prodigal son—the story both about the one who's so lavish in expenditure, and then an unforgiving brother and a very interesting father who would if he could, try to reconcile them—what provokes that story is the way in which some of the Pharisees and the scribes were, according to the text, murmuring against the practice that Jesus himself had of eating with tax collectors and others who were regarded as sinners. This is described in the 15th chapter of the Gospel of Luke. Without Jesus ever needing so much as to mention it in so many words, the opposing parties are like the two brothers of the parable and they are at odds.

According to the story, the younger brother gets his father to give him an advance, his share of the inheritance and then he runs off to squander it on a life of wine and women and song. Why, he seems like the very embodiment of a freedom to enjoy life away from authority and all the normal network of social relations; a kind of freedom that hasn't been matched until the modern generation of college freshmen. At Fordham, I live among college freshmen and they love their freedom.

The license to do what he liked, however, in this story, proves a very empty form of liberty, when suddenly all his possessions are gone. Maybe you know Dickens's story, *Great Expectations*, but there's a character there, Mr. Wemmick, who likes to talk about portable property, what you can carry with you. Well, this young man, all of his property is now gone. He's spent it very foolishly and it is only in this moment of abject poverty to which his false freedom has led him, that now suddenly he can hear the voice of conscience and I'd like to read that portion of the parable because it's just a remarkable passage. I'm starting around verse 17 in chapter 15:

> But when he came to himself he said, "How many of my father's hired servants have bread enough and to spare, but I perish here with hunger! I will arise and go to my father, and I will say to him, 'Father, I have sinned against heaven and before you; I am no longer worthy to be called your son; treat me as one of your hired servants.'"

What I hear in that part of the story is the young man's conscience bothering him. Within his conscience, the young man realizes that he really does need to repent his offense against his father and he's hoping, if not for forgiveness, he's hoping at least to get a position in his father's household so that he can work like one of the hired hands. His father, however, has been watching for his wayward son from a long way off, looking and hoping against hope. He doesn't even give the young man a chance to deliver the whole of the speech he's been practicing. I mean, when I try to imagine this story I think of the young man saying it about 25 times on the walk back. He's been practicing it so he'll deliver it perfectly. Instead, the father comes out and kisses him and embraces him, directs the fatted calf to be killed for a feast to welcome back the prodigal son.

In this way the father in the story acts in the very pattern of God as we so often saw him in the Old Testament. I think, for example, of the way in which God is shown in Hosea, who takes Israel back after all the infidelities that have broken the marital covenant. Let me maybe even just quote for a line or two from that. Looking in particular at Hosea 11:

> How can I give you up, O Ephraim! How can I hand you
>   over, O Israel!
> How can I make you like Admah! How can I treat you
>   like Zeboim!
> My heart recoils within me, my compassion grows warm
>   and tender.
> I will not execute my fierce anger, I will not again
>   destroy Ephraim;
> for I am God and not man, the Holy One in your midst,
> and I will not come to destroy.

What I find to be the most fascinating turn in this story is the next part. The resentment of the elder brother who is angered by the apparently all too easy forgiveness the prodigal son receives from his father. In the rant that he then makes to his father about the injustice of it all, he not only understands nothing of the conversion that has occurred within his brother, but he cannot even see fit to call this interloper by the very name of brother. I'm up to verses 29 and 30 of chapter 15 of Luke:

> Lo, these many years I have served you, and I never disobeyed your command; yet you never game me a kid, that I might make merry with my friends. But when this son of yours came, who has devoured your living with harlots, you killed for him the fatted calf!

Well, the parable ends with the father explaining what his fidelity means. He says, "Son, you're always with me, and all that is mine is yours." In no way does the father dispute the fidelity that the older brother has shown, but he does remind him about the joy that is only right for us to have when a sinner repents. We should delight in giving and receiving when we see it; we don't have to be in on it. The parable doesn't explain how the elder brother reacts. It doesn't explain what's in store for the younger brother when the party is over. I must admit that I suspect that he'll have some time working in the mail room for awhile before he gets to return to the board room and help run the family business again.

The text of Luke, instead, moves on to other parables. We get the parable of the dishonest steward in chapter 16. We get the case of Lazarus and Dives a little bit later in chapter 16. Both of them also bear on the situation that was right then before Jesus in the person of the Pharisees and the tax collectors. For our purposes, right now, simply in considering how Jesus uses parables for his own distinctive pattern of wisdom teaching, I think the point is presumably quite clear. There is need for justice and there is need for mercy. Not only are justice and mercy not opposed, they are both necessary. There is no excuse for injustice and the rupture of social relations that's involved in sin must be restored. But equally prominent in his message is this, the wisdom of forgiveness; not only in being ready to bestow forgiveness, but in learning how best to receive it and where we stand if we're a third party, learning how to rejoice in it rather than to be jealous or envious or self-righteous.

In my judgment, the parables are fundamental to the divine perspective of Christ's wisdom. They present the message in unforgettable ways. In the next lecture, we will turn to another way in which Jesus is wisdom teacher; namely in some of his famous sermons and I'll look in particular at the Sermon on the Mount.

Lecture Thirty-Five
Jesus and the Sermon on the Mount

Scope:

We have seen that one of the most important aspects of biblical wisdom literature is its ethical dimension, often as connected to the problem of innocent suffering and the rectification of injustice. This lecture will concentrate on the Sermon on the Mount as the paradigmatic instance of Jesus as wisdom teacher. It will examine his presentation of the Beatitudes, including the echoes of earlier portions of biblical wisdom literature in these sayings, and analyze the structure of the rest of the Sermon on the Mount in light of the traditional questions and concerns of biblical wisdom literature in the areas of virtues and vices, the gifts of divine grace, and the summons for the proper use of human freedom in response.

Outline

I. The Sermon on the Mount.

    A. After the arrest of John the Baptist, the Gospel of Matthew presents a very short account of the beginnings of Jesus's public ministry with a focus on the message "Repent, for the kingdom of heaven is at hand" (4:17) and the calling of the first disciples.

    B. Immediately following that, we have three chapters that present the Sermon on the Mount (5:1–7:27), in which Jesus appears as a wisdom teacher—one in the tradition of Moses and Solomon, but greater than they, with the special authority that comes from his divinity as the Son of God.

    C. In choosing to go up onto a mountain and sit as his disciples surround him, Jesus assumes the posture of teaching authority, presumably with allusion to rabbis who teach from the chair of Moses but as one who gives this teaching to everyone who will accept his teaching and become his disciple.

    D. The major parts of this discourse are as follows:

        1. The Beatitudes (5:3–12).

        2. Proclaiming a renewal of Torah and an authoritative interpretation (5:17–48).

3. Practical applications: new and old (6:1–34).

4. Examples: freshness and continuity (7:1–27).

II. Jesus as a new Moses and a new Solomon.

   A. It is a mistake, I think, to present the Beatitudes as if they replaced the Decalogue with some new teaching that is discontinuous with the Torah. Nowhere does Jesus do anything other than affirm the 10 Commandments.

   B. If anything, the Beatitudes echo the kind of blessings promised in some of the texts that we have studied, such as Psalm 1, which begins by calling "blessed" or "happy" those who obey the law of God.

   C. The Beatitudes that follow list the conditions for those who would be the disciples of Jesus, and in fact they give a picture of Jesus himself.

III. Some further detail.

   A. In Luke's version, the first Beatitude reads: "Blessed are you poor, for yours is the kingdom of God" (Luke 6:20b), while Matthew has it "Blessed are the poor in spirit, for theirs is the kingdom of heaven" (Matthew 5:3).

   B. What Christians have long comprehended from this passage is the need for coming to see that one's riches are not one's salvation. What is required instead is vigorous work for justice, both individually and socially, and for charity in taking care of the needs of the poor.

   C. When the second Beatitude speaks of mourning, it is sometimes taken to be referring to mourning over the death of dear ones whom we have lost, but there is also a long tradition of taking it to refer rather to mourning for our sins. In short, we must endure pain in bidding farewell to that which is wrong or wicked and yet we have loved or gotten used to it.

   D. The third Beatitude echoes Psalm 37 [36]:11. Once again, there may be an allusion here to the *anawim* who were left behind on the land when Judah's conquerors carted off the elite to exile in Babylon. It could also evoke the figure of Moses, and it is certainly a portrait of Christ himself.

E. We could meditate with profit on each of the other Beatitudes in much the same way, but for the purposes of considering the whole of the Sermon on the Mount as Jesus's wisdom address, let us turn briefly to the rest of his discourse.

IV. The Torah of the Messiah.

  A. The other three parts of the sermon (5:17–7:27) present the law of Christ. One can see a number of the writings of Saint Paul—for instance, in both Romans and Galatians—as efforts to understand and explain the doctrine that is presented here.

  B. While the parts of the law that deal with ritual, ceremony, and custom are subject to change, the core that is the Decalogue is entirely preserved.

  C. In the course of the sermon, the wisdom teaching that Jesus does includes his authoritative interpretation of what some of the commandments of the Decalogue entail. We also learn a pattern of prayer.

  D. While asserting the authority to modify disciplinary aspects of the ceremonial part of the law, Jesus deepens our understanding of the Decalogue.

  E. The Sermon on the Mount even includes a brief reference to the covenant with Noah that we discussed in connection with the problem of the suffering of the innocent.

  F. The ethical demands that are specified here and throughout the sermon will severely try anyone's resources—in fact, they will presumably exceed everyone's native resources.

  G. Within the Sermon on the Mount, this same point is made when Jesus teaches his disciples the prayer that we know as the LORD's Prayer, or the Our Father. Like the psalms that we saw to be deeply connected with other parts of wisdom literature, we should see its seven petitions as prayers for the grace needed to accept the wisdom teaching of Jesus, to ask for the graces we need, and to be ready even for difficult tasks like the requirement of being ready to forgive if we expect to be forgiven.

Suggested Reading:

Benedict XVI, *Jesus of Nazareth*, esp. chap. 5.

Pinckaers, *The Sources of Christian Ethics*.

Questions to Consider:

1. How do you understand the Beatitudes: as ideals or as obligations of the Christian life?

2. The Gospels contain many discussions of forgiveness in addition to the important lines on this subject in the LORD's Prayer. How, for instance, do you understand the discussion between Jesus and Peter about the need to forgive not just 7 times but 70 times 7 times and the accompanying parable about the master and the debtor? (See Matthew 18:21–35.)

3. What is distinctive about Jesus's way of handling the question of innocent suffering in his allusion to the covenant with Noah (God makes the sun to rise on the evil and the good and sends rain on the just and the unjust alike)?

Lecture Thirty-Five—Transcript
Jesus and the Sermon on the Mount

In the course of these lectures, we have seen that one of the most import aspects of biblical wisdom literature is its ethical dimension, often as connected to the problem of innocent suffering and the rectification of injustice. This lecture will concentrate on the Sermon on the Mount as the paradigmatic instance of Jesus as wisdom teacher, focusing especially on those ethical questions. It will examine his presentation of the Beatitudes, including the echoes of earlier portions of biblical wisdom literature that is found in these sayings. And it will analyze the structure of the rest of the Sermon on the Mount in light of the traditional questions and concerns of biblical wisdom literature in the area of virtues and vices, the gifts of divine grace, and the summons for proper use of human freedom in response.

Let's take a look then at the Sermon on the Mount beginning with a consideration of its context. After the arrest of John the Baptist, according to the Gospel of Matthew, there is a very short account of the beginnings of Jesus's public ministry. This is chapter 4 beginning around verse 12 and there's a certain focus on the message, "Repent, for the kingdom of heaven is at hand." You'll find that find in verse 17. There's also the calling of the first disciples.

Immediately following that in the text, we have three chapters that present the Sermon on the Mount. It begins with chapter 5, verse 1 and goes through the end of chapter 7, in which Jesus appears as a wisdom teacher, someone in the tradition of Moses and Solomon. And yet it presents him as greater than they with that special authority that comes from his divinity as the very Son of God. In choosing to go up on a mountain to deliver this sermon and then to sit as his disciples surround him, Jesus assumes the posture of teaching authority. Presumably, his very body posture is an allusion to rabbis who taught from the chair of Moses. One hears a reference to that in the Gospel of Matthew chapter 23, verse 2 and yet, he's also one who gives this teaching to everyone who will accept it; to anyone who will become his disciple. It's a teaching which does not come from mere human learning, but one who speaks from the very place where he's busying praying; namely, he's praying to his Father and he speaks from the mountain, like the voice that Moses heard on Mount Sinai, one whose covenant will embrace the whole world.

Let's turn also to a consideration of the structure of the discourse; it has a number of very distinct parts. First, there are the Beatitudes; that's chapter 5, verses 3–12. The next part is his proclamation that what he's doing is a renewal of Torah and giving it an authentic interpretation; that's the rest of chapter 5. The third part is some practical applications, both new ones and old ones. One finds that in the entirety of chapter 6 and then finally, chapter 7 is about examples. I find that those examples manifest both freshness, as well as, a continuity with what has gone before.

There's actually a briefer version of this same material, usually because it's set differently, it's set on a plain instead of on a mountain. It's called the Sermon on the Plain. That's found in the sixth chapter of Luke from verse 17 all the way up to verse 49 and there are a couple of differences. For example, instead of the eight beatitudes that we'll find in the Gospel of Matthew, the Sermon on the Plain has a set of four beatitudes expressed just a little differently, and then four admonitions; woe is, woe is. The whole of the Gospel of Luke is admittedly directed to the Gentiles rather than to the Jews as the audience. And I suspect that it may be precisely for this reason that the focus in Luke's account of this material is not so much on Jesus as delivering the definitive interpretation of Torah, that's what we find in Matthew, but rather as explaining the demands of discipleship that will have to be met by anyone, Gentile or Jew, who wants to join him.

When we turn then to the content of this, I think what we see is Jesus in the person of a new Moses and a new Solomon. Let's begin by taking a look at chapter 5 and the account of the Beatitudes. I think that it's a mistake to present the Beatitudes as if they replaced the Decalogue with some new teaching that is discontinuous with Torah. Nowhere does Jesus do anything other than affirm the Ten Commandments. One might want to look at the parallel passages in Mark 10:19, in Luke 16:17; so too here. As we have already seen, he clearly states within the Sermon on the Mount that he has not come to abolish the Law and the Prophets, but rather has come to fulfill them. If anything, the Beatitudes echo the very kind of blessings that were promised in some of the texts that we've studied earlier in this series; Psalm 1 for example, when it begins by calling blessed or happy are those who obey the Law of God and then talks about their blessings. Likewise, throughout the sapiential literature, we have seen the invocation of blessings on those who fear the LORD. It was a very strong theme.

The Beatitudes that then follow here in the text of the Sermon on the Mount list the conditions for those who would become the disciples of Jesus; this is what they have to do. In fact, I think they give us a picture of Jesus himself, sort of as a character study. I see them as in some ways, very similar to Proverbs and to Sirach as well as to the figure of King Solomon in the book that we were studying called the Wisdom of Solomon, in that they lay out how true disciples are to conduct themselves, even while they're busy giving assurance that God will provide for them, even in the worst of their troubles.

Some of them, of course, are very counterintuitive. Who would ever think that being poor, whether in actual poverty or poverty of spirit, who would ever think that being poor is a blessing? There have been figures in the history of thought—I think of Nietzsche, for example—Nietzsche simply railed at Jesus for calling the meek blessed. To say that being persecuted is a blessing strikes many people as being uttered ironically. Let's consider them in some detail; I'll begin by just reading the text of the Beatitudes and then we can discuss them:

> Blessed are the poor in spirit, for theirs is the kingdom
>   of heaven.
> Blessed are those who mourn, for they shall be comforted.
> Blessed are the meek, for they shall inherit the earth.
> Blessed are those who hunger and thirst for righteousness,
>   for they shall be satisfied.
> Blessed are the merciful, for they shall obtain mercy.
> Blessed are the pure in heart, for they shall see God.
> Blessed are the peacemakers, for they shall be called sons
>   of God.
> Blessed are those who are persecuted for righteousness'
>   sake, for theirs is the kingdom of heaven.
> Blessed are you when men revile you and persecute you
>   and utter all kinds of evil against you falsely on my
>   account. Rejoice and be glad, for your reward is great in
>   heaven, for so men persecuted the prophets who were
>   before you.

That was the text from Matthew. While it will not be possible here to deal with everything that this text mentions, I think it will be profitable for our purposes to select a couple of the items and consider them in further detail.

In Luke's version of this, the very first beatitude reads slightly differently, "Blessed are you poor, for yours is the kingdom of God." The way that Matthew has it in the text I just read is, "Blessed are the poor in spirit, for theirs is the kingdom of heaven." Well, in addition to the difference between direct and indirect address, namely one says yours the other says theirs, there's also the difference between poor and poor in spirit. What do we make of that?

Presumably this phrase alludes to the faithful remnant who were left behind in Israel after the deportation of the people to Babylon. At least that's how it's used in Zephaniah chapter 3, verses 12–19, that they're so frequently described as the faithful in the Psalms, waiting for God's salvation. I presume that it's something like that here, that there's the thought of those who are faithful even if they're a remnant. This is the ones to whom God is making a promise.

There are some who see Matthew's version as trying to spiritualize what Luke had presented as simple material poverty. Those who see it that way sometimes think that this is impoverishing the radical nature of Jesus's doctrine here. I don't agree with that interpretation. That interpretation doesn't seem at all to me to fit with Luke's own frequent attention to the inner demands of Christian discipleship and I suspect that when Matthew is using "poor in spirit," he's talking more about those *anawim*, about the poor remnant. Further, it is important to remember that material poverty alone is not what brings about holiness or salvation. Material poverty can be an incentive to think about it but there is still need for an action of the spirit and for an action of grace. For Christ, what is required in both rich and poor alike is that we turn our hearts back to God. That's all the way through the Gospels and for this reason, Jesus, he has some very hard things to say about riches. One will find that if you look at, say the Gospel of Mark chapter 10, starting around verse 17, that's the place where he makes that very interesting assertion, that it is easier for a camel to pass through the eye of a needle than for the rich to enter heaven.

What Christians have long comprehended from this passage is the need to come to see that one's riches are not themselves one's salvation. What is required instead is vigorous work for justice, individually and socially in cooperation with others, and a strong need for charity in taking care of the needs of the poor. One way to approach this has been to cultivate an attitude that regards the goods of this world not as one's own possessions, but rather, as means and instruments that have been given to us and whose proper use needs to be determined by a project of seeing how they can serve to promote Christ's kingdom. Any number of saints have reflected on this and dwelt on it and I think that they've got a better interpretation there.

Let's turn now to the second beatitude, "Blessed are those who mourn, for they shall be comforted." It speaks of mourning. Presumably when it does, it needs to be interpreted, mourning in what sense. Sometimes it's taken to refer to mourning over the death of our dear ones whom we have lost. And then presumably the consolation that is mentioned refers to the comfort that we will have in seeing them again in eternity, just as those who mourned the death of Jesus did see him again after the resurrection and he promises that we too will rise. But there is also a long tradition of taking that second beatitude not so much to refer to the mourning over someone who is dead, but mourning for our sins; in short, the pain that we must endure in bidding farewell to what is wrong or what is wicked, even though we love it and even though we've gotten used to it. There is an unbelievable comfort that comes when one has repented one's sins, when one has been forgiven and when one is living anew and aright, at peace with God. So I suspect that quite likely the interpretation of that second beatitude refers to, if you mourn your sins there will be comfort given.

The third beatitude, "Blessed are the meek, for they shall inherit the earth," echoes Psalm 37, especially verse 11 which reads, "But the meek shall possess the land and delight themselves in abundant prosperity." I think there's a biblical echo there directly from the Psalms. There may be here also an allusion to the *anawim*, those who were left behind, the faithful on the land when Judah's conquerors carted off the elite over to exile in Babylon. It could also be that what we're evoking here is the figure of Moses. I think back to a passage such as the book of Numbers 12:3, which regards the meek as, more than anyone else on the face of the earth, important. It is certainly a portrait of Christ himself, whom Matthew 11: 29–30 describes in this way, "Take my yoke upon you, and learn from me; for I am gentle and lowly [or meek] in heart, and you will find rest for your souls.

For my yoke is easy and my burden is light." In that way one sees the Beatitudes as not only giving advice, but really recommending to us a picture of Jesus.

We could very well meditate with profit on each of the other beatitudes in much this same way. They are promises made for those who hunger for justice, for the merciful, for the pure in heart, for the peacemakers, for those who are persecuted for righteousness, for those who are reviled for their fidelity to Christ. But for the purpose of considering the whole of the Sermon on the Mount as Jesus's wisdom address, let's now turn, at least briefly, to the rest of the discourse.

The next part is something that I call the Torah of the Messiah. There are three other parts that we need to consider here from chapter 5, verse 17, all the way to the end of chapter 7, and what they do is present the law of Christ and then give examples. One can see a number of writings elsewhere in the New Testament in a similar vein. For instance, there are parts of St. Paul that try to understand and explain the very doctrine that's presented here. He does this throughout the letter to the Romans and throughout the letter to the Galatians. While parts of the Torah that deal with ritual and ceremony and custom are subject to change, there is a core, the Decalogue, that is entirely preserved. I'm referring to those parts of the law which deal with food laws and purity laws and circumcision laws and the laws dealing with the Sabbath.

Well, when Jesus handles that in various places, he always distinguishes between the ritual laws and the core that is the Decalogue. You might want to take a look, for instance, at the Gospel of Mark, chapter 7, starting at around verse 14. The core does not change but admittedly, the ritual laws can be changed. For Jesus, it is not physical descent from Abraham, but faith that ultimately matters, not physical kinship in the community but rather, individuals who are from peoples and nations that are even entirely unrelated to Judaism. They may be adopted as the brothers and sisters of Jesus and thereby made the adopted children of God. Admittedly, this is a change in understanding it. This is the freshness or the newness, the difference and not just the continuity. Christians have understood this part of Jesus's teaching to be what happens through baptism. We become the brothers and sisters of Jesus, the adopted children of God.

In the course of the Sermon, the wisdom that Jesus teaches does include his authoritative interpretation of what some of the commandments of the Decalogue entail. We're also going to hear a certain pattern of prayer. While asserting the authority to modify certain disciplinary aspects of the ceremonial part of the law, Jesus also works on deepening our understanding of the Decalogue. In fact, in the tradition of the holiness code that is found in Leviticus, the part of Leviticus from chapter 17 through chapter 26, Jesus insists that what the commandments require is not merely some external action, but a rightness of the heart. For example, here in the Sermon on the Mount, chapter 5, verses 21 through about 26, in which Jesus reads the commandment that forbids murder, also to forbid holding our sister or our brother, anyone, in contempt. Or chapter 5 starting at around verse 27, Jesus explains that to look lustfully at a woman who is not one's spouse is already to have committed adultery with her in one's heart.

The requirement for mercy also receives his special attention. I'd like to suggest that we read a little bit of that because again, it's so powerful in terms of his own teaching of a certain ethic. This is the part that begins at chapter 5 verse 38:

> You have heard that it was said, "Eye for an eye and a tooth for a tooth." But I say to you, Do not resist one who is evil. But if anyone strikes you on the right cheek, turn to him the other also; and if anyone would sue you and take your coat, let him have your cloak as well; and if anyone forces you to go one mile, go with him two miles. Give to him who begs from you, and do not refuse him who would borrow from you.

The Sermon on the Mount even includes a brief reference to the covenant with Noah that we discussed in connection with the problem of the suffering of the innocent when we were dealing with Proverbs and Job. That is, it makes a strong ethical teaching and it connects it with the covenant. But as we saw, the connection with the covenant has to be very alert to, what stage in the covenant, and we saw so much interesting material as we were going along when those allusions to Noah would come up and there's another one coming here. Jesus treats it as an abiding condition of the human existence, that the good and the wicked do have to live together. But the wisdom that he brings to this discussion, a divine wisdom, is that we need to imitate God's ways of loving and thereby to somehow grow perfect. Again, let me read that part of it. This is chapter 5, beginning with verse 43:

> You have heard that it was said, "You shall love your neighbor and hate your enemy." But I say to you, Love your enemies and pray for those who persecute you, so that you may be sons of your Father who is in heaven, for he makes his sun rise on the evil and on the good and sends rain on the just and on the unjust. For if you love those who love you, what reward have you? Do not even the tax collectors do the same? And if you salute only your brethren, what more are you doing than others? Do not even the Gentiles do the same? You, therefore, must be perfect, as your heavenly Father is perfect.

What we've got there of course, is that allusion to Noah. It kept coming up as we were doing the earlier parts of biblical wisdom literature because of the way in which it changes the expectation. No longer would there be an immediate retribution, that there would be an immediate payback for the good we do or an immediate punishment for the wickedness that we do, but rather, a sense that rich and poor, that good and bad, that all of these need to live together and that this is in a way a part of the way in which God gives us freedom. Our actions will have our consequences. God will take care of it in the long run.

Well, some of that is here, an expectation that freedom is the condition in which we live and yet, there are also ethical demands. The ethical demands that are specified here and throughout the Sermon on the Mount will surely try anyone's resources severely. In fact, I think Jesus is clear; they will presumably exceed our native resources. Quite relevant here to the fact that this can seem to be too much, that any of the things that Jesus described in the Beatitudes or that Jesus has been talking about here, for example, that opening gambit in the last passage, love your enemies, do good to those who persecute you.

Very relevant to understanding how we're supposed to do that is a passage from a little bit later in Matthew. Admittedly, it's beyond the text of the Sermon on the Mount, but I think it's also highly relevant for the understanding of Jesus as wisdom teacher and it's another one of those stories. It's the story of the rich young man who wants to know what more he needs to do to have eternal life, in addition to keeping the commandments. He tells Jesus he's already kept them. When Jesus tells him that what he has to do is to sell all that he has and give it to the poor and then come and follow Jesus as a disciple, the young man goes away sad. Well, when the disciples see the young man go away sad, figuring that he just doesn't have the resources, he doesn't have the strength to do what Jesus is telling him, the disciples are really perplexed and they're wondering, how in the world is anyone ever going to be saved? They might well be wondering, how are they going to be saved? And so they ask Jesus, how is this possible? Jesus answers in a word—this is Matthew 19: 26—"With men it is impossible, but with God all things are possible." What Christian theologians have understood about Jesus's wisdom teaching from that answer is that we do have an indispensable need for grace. Yes, we're supposed to rely upon our own resources. Yes, we ought to be trained in the virtues, we ought to be trained to avoid the vices, and that the point of a good education in these moral virtues, that a good education of conscience where we're quite clear on what it is that the new law demands and what it is that the Decalogue demands and the fullness, the interiorization of that teaching. But that we should never think that the statement of the law or the knowledge of morality or this set of directives is entirely a matter of our own doing. It's a matter, rather, of our cooperation with grace.

Well, as you remember when we were considering the text from the Wisdom of Solomon, when the very figure of Solomon was instructing his fellow kings of the earth about the need to know where wisdom is and to pray deeply for wisdom so that they can observe the moral law, so that they can be the kind of kings who would be truly just and be truly serving the common good, Solomon had instructed them on their need to pray. Here at the conclusion of the Sermon on the Mount in exactly that pattern, Jesus also makes the same point with his disciples because what he urges his disciples is that they vigorously need to pray for the grace, and what we find him doing is teaching the disciples the central prayer that is typical of Jesus; the prayer that we often refer to as the LORD's Prayer or the Our Father. Like the psalms that we saw in a couple of these lectures to be so deeply connected with wisdom literature, we should see the seven petitions of the LORD's Prayer as prayers, each step by step, prayers for the grace needed to accept the wisdom teaching of Jesus;

to ask for the graces that we need to carry it out in life and even to be ready for the difficult tasks, like that task of needing to be ready to forgive if we expect to be forgiven.

Let's turn here at the conclusion of this particular lecture to the words of that prayer and again, I'll use the words of the Revised Standard Version translation:

> Our Father, who art in heaven, hallowed be thy name.
> Thy kingdom come,
> Thy will be done,
> on earth as it is in heaven.
> Give us this day our daily bread,
> And forgive us our debts,
> As we also have forgiven our debtors;
> And lead us not into temptation,
> But deliver us from evil.

In a passage like that where we are hearing the words that Jesus recommends to us for prayer, we're also learning from him some of the content and learning how to pray for precisely that grace we need. One could very well ask, for instance, about that passage about forgive us our debts—or our trespasses, as another translation has it—forgive us our trespasses as we have forgiven trespasses against us. It really requires that we reflect for a bit on our own practice and if we've been generous in it, then we can pray with all the more fervor and all the more integrity and all the more earnestness that we ourselves be forgiven.

The wisdom of Jesus is, I think, contained in a prayer like that here at the conclusion on the Sermon on the Mount, where he has been so eager to provide us with a teaching in clarity, but then also mindful that it may seem too hard or may seem beyond us. He gives us his own direct indication in such great continuity with the rest of wisdom literature that we need to pray for the strength to do that.

In the next lecture, we will try to sum up the themes of this course. We've been through the Old Testament and New and now it's going to be time to take a look at what we've learned by surveying the course as a whole.

Lecture Thirty-Six
Overview of Biblical Wisdom Literature

Scope:

This lecture reviews the main themes of the course, beginning with the place of the sapiential books within the Bible and then reflecting on the question of what "wisdom" means within biblical wisdom literature. We will focus on three areas of significance: wisdom as divine wisdom (what God wants teach us); wisdom as what nature, cosmos, and creatures have to teach us; and wisdom as human wisdom (the understanding achieved through human effort about human nature and human behavior).

Outline

I. Wisdom literature as part of the Bible.

    A. The effort to understand the traditions of divine revelation that are involved in Judaism and Christianity necessarily involves coming to know the scriptures.

    B. Both the synagogue and the church have sophisticated ideas about which texts make up the Bible. They share a reverence for the Torah, for the Prophets, and for other writings such as the Psalms and the sapiential literature that we have been studying in this course.

    C. What Christianity recognizes as the biblical New Testament stands in a profound continuity with what came before, whether we think of this as the Hebrew Bible or as the Old Testament (and thus a canon that includes a few additional documents that are not in Hebrew but are connected to the chosen people of Israel).

    D. The sapiential books are an important part of the Bible. They are in some respects different in kind from the others but in many respects deeply connected to the rest.

II. What does "wisdom" mean?

    A. The texts of biblical wisdom literature give us this first sense of "wisdom" very strongly in the many assertions that the covenant and the law are divine wisdom.

B. It is wisdom for orienting one's life: that, above all, adoration and praise is owed to God.

C. It is likewise wisdom for living one's daily life. The second tablet of the Decalogue not only spells out individual duties and prohibitions but also provides a pattern for peaceful life within a community.

D. An important sense of "wisdom" here is the notion of what we can come to understand by looking at what God has made: the cosmos as a whole, the nature of various creatures in the cosmos, and human nature in particular.

E. While biblical wisdom literature does not offer us a systematic picture of the cosmos or the natures of various creatures in the way that philosophy and the sciences have tried to do, there is nonetheless respect for that type of inquiry.

F. Connected to the second sense of "wisdom," and especially to the concern about knowledge of human nature, is a third distinct sense of "wisdom" as human wisdom.

G. There is also the wisdom that comes from questioning—in fact, from pressing hard questions to the limits of one's imagination. The book of Job strikes me as exemplifying this sense of "wisdom."

H. These are questions that come readily to the human heart, and the Bible's sapiential literature gives voice to those questions and then really debates them, and really invites us to join the debate.

I. To provide compassion may mean readying ourselves to offer personal care and real help to those in suffering. This too is something about which we need to have practical wisdom.

J. It is erroneous to think that all suffering is a payback for guilt, and in this Job's friends need to be corrected. What they should be praised for is their compassion in sitting and accompanying their friend.

III. Prayer and reflection.

    A. As interludes during our course, we turned from time to time to the Psalter and considered a number of psalms that are collectively called the wisdom psalms. These are forms of prayer that are open to believer and to searcher alike.

    B. Happily, the poetry of the Hebrew psalms is based not on rhythm or rhyme but on balance and opposition, and so these psalms are easily translatable into any language. They are a prayer book for religious communities and individuals, for believers and those who are still searching.

    C. In the Wisdom of Solomon, the figure of King Solomon shows the wisdom for which he is known, in my judgment, when he informs his fellow kings that his reputation for wisdom is not simply the result of his native abilities. Rather, he asserts, it is a gift that he has received. He then reminds his colleagues of the need that he had to pray for wisdom, and he shows them a way in which to do so.

    D. Whatever our individual abilities or accomplishments or experiences, there is the need to be receptive for wisdom to grow. Part of that receptivity means leaving time in our lives for reflection, and being open to assistance. There is good reason to follow Solomon's example in raising mind and heart in prayer, asking for the gift of wisdom.

    E. Allow me a personal note here at the end of the course, to thank you for joining me on this journey through biblical wisdom literature. I hope that it has been helpful to you, and I wish you blessings as you continue this journey.

Suggested Reading:

Duggan, *The Consuming Fire*.

Von Rad, *Wisdom in Israel*.

Wiesenthal, *The Sunflower*.

Questions to Consider:

1. Having now considered many biblical texts on the problem of suffering, how do you see the question? Is it correct to say that suffering is inescapable in a world in which there are free creatures?

2. All considered, what is the relation between Torah and wisdom? How does the covenant between God and the chosen people bear on the question of wisdom?

3. Who are the people in your life whom you especially esteem as wise? Where does their wisdom seem to come from? Do they fit into the three categories suggested here?

Lecture Thirty-Six—Transcript
Overview of Biblical Wisdom Literature

This lecture reviews the main themes for the whole of our course. We'll begin with the place of the sapiential books within the Bible and then use for our reflection this question: what does wisdom mean within biblical wisdom literature? We'll focus in particular on three areas of significance: wisdom as divine wisdom, what God wants to teach us; wisdom as what nature, cosmos and creature have to teach us; and wisdom as human wisdom, the understanding achieved through human effort about human nature and human behavior.

So, my question is, are you ready for the final exam? Just kidding! It is time, however, in this final lecture of the series to ask ourselves some questions. What conclusions can we draw from our study? What lessons have we learned? As with other courses that are offered by The Teaching Company, you might want to do this as an exercise for yourself on paper or in discussion; what have you learned, as well as by listening to this lecture while I try to crystallize what I think we've been learning by our discussion. I'll attempt to get the process started first, by reviewing the place of biblical wisdom literature within the Bible and then secondly, I'll try to consider that question about what wisdom is that I asked a moment ago.

The effort to understand the traditions of divine revelation that are involved within Judaism and within Christianity necessarily involves coming to know the scriptures; reading the Bible and pondering it. Both the synagogue and the church have extremely sophisticated ideas about which texts make up the Bible. They share a reverence for Torah, for the Prophets and for the other writings, such as the Psalms, and much of the sapiential literature that we have been studying in this course.

What Christianity recognizes as the biblical New Testament stands in a profound continuity with what came before. Whether we think of that "what came before" as the Hebrew Bible or as the Old Testament and thus, especially if you see the phrase Old Testament, a canon that includes a few additional documents that for the Orthodox Church and for the Catholic Church, are not in Hebrew but are nonetheless very deeply connected to the chosen people of Israel by their origin and by their object. In that material too, there are various elements that are in the wisdom tradition, such as some of the sayings and the sermons of Jesus within the Gospels as well as some of the sapiential books that I was discussing, for example, Sirach and the Wisdom of Solomon.

The sapiential books are an important part of the Bible. In some respects, they are different in kind from the others. On the other hand, there are many ways in which they are just very deeply connected. Let me try to review that.

The books of biblical wisdom literature are not primarily historical. They're not primarily a historical record of God's people but from time to time they do touch on history, as when, for instance, Sirach turns to the ranks of the patriarchs for inspirational examples of virtue or again, when the Wisdom of Solomon reflects on the plagues that are sent upon the Egyptians. It does so in order to illustrate the proactive role of divine providence and give us a sense about how divine wisdom works. Another consideration, the books of the biblical wisdom literature tradition are not the texts that are of the primary display of the Decalogue; they're not the main way in which legislation is codified. But they do regularly advert to the central biblical idea of covenant as absolutely essential to a life of wisdom, precisely because wisdom requires right relationship to God and it is by the covenant that God has established the pattern for such right relationship. It's only by meditating on covenant, understanding it deeply, that we can be in that right relationship and the books of wisdom literature do it as much and as well as any other part of the Bible.

A third area of consideration, the books of biblical wisdom literature do not contain the magisterial pronouncements of the prophets with all their characteristic formulas such as, "The LORD says that ..." and it goes on, but in their more philosophical tenor, in their way of engaging with the pressing questions about how to live one's life, how to deal with suffering, how to understand what doesn't seem to make sense. They regularly return to a notion that is deeply important to the prophets, namely that fear of the LORD is the beginning of wisdom. The prophets reemphasize and teach that again and again too.

Let's turn to the other question that I asked as a way to integrate our material and to synthesize what we've been learning: What does wisdom mean? If we reflect on the materials that we have studied during this course, I think that we will come to the conclusion that in a phrase like biblical wisdom literature, the term wisdom refers to the understanding, the knowledge, the good sense, the insight, that comes ultimately from God, but that is accessible to us in various ways, by receiving the wisdom that God offers and by thinking things through for ourselves.

I would propose that we'll make best sense of this if we list three senses for the term wisdom. First, wisdom as what God would teach us; second, wisdom as what nature, what cosmos, what the various creatures that make up the natural world have to teach us; and third, wisdom as truly and immediately human understanding. That is, a knowledge of human nature, a knowledge of human behavior, a knowledge of human community. Let's deal with each of those three in turn.

First, wisdom as what God would teach us. I think that the texts of biblical wisdom literature give us this first sense of wisdom very strongly, especially in those many assertions that covenant and the Law really do constitute divine wisdom. That the way God has set up the covenant and the way in which God continued to reinforce it and sometimes even to deepen it and to make it more demanding and the way in which God has put together the Law, the Torah; this is divine wisdom. How often Israel prays in thanksgiving for the great gift that is the Law, that it's a special gift that was given to no other people. That's appreciating the Law, the covenant as wisdom.

It is a wisdom for orienting one's life; that is, above all other things, adoration and praise are owed to God. One should not think that other peoples have their own gods but somehow should regard other alleged deities as simply false claimants to the title of God. Those aren't true gods and that that's a part of what the Law has to say. Likewise, the Law includes the notion that on the LORD's Day, on the Sabbath, one should refrain from the normal chores of work and business, but one should truly honor God. One should be with one's family as far as possible, and even by one's rest one should imitate God who, after all, was described in Genesis as resting after six days of the work of Creation.

Likewise, it is wisdom for living one's daily life. When one thinks of the Decalogue, the Ten Commandments, often one thinks about them as in two tablets. One tablet pertaining to our obligations to God; a second tablet as indicating our obligations to our fellow human beings. The second tablet of the Decalogue spells out not just individual duties and individual prohibitions, but it provides a pattern for peaceful life within a community—honoring one's parents in all the senses of honoring parents, not killing or committing adultery or stealing or bearing false witness—in all of the ways in which those things are meant, not just in a limited legalistic minimalist way, but understanding all of what's involved. There is even reference in the final injunctions of the Decalogue to disciplining one's desires and one's will by the prohibition on coveting another's spouse, coveting another's goods. It strikes me as something deeply wise to have this restraint upon our wayward thoughts lest those wayward thoughts turn into wayward deeds.

A second main way in which to see the sapiential literature as conveying divine wisdom is to appreciate the way in which all of these books are in the sphere of revelation and inspiration. Even if the texts were written down by human authors, they're guided by a divine source. For example, some of them, as we saw in our considerations of the Song of Songs, they really give evidence that we have to think about diverse levels of meaning here; that is, that there's an entire level of meaning that goes beyond the literal meaning about an interesting human love story, to another meaning that is above that but is intended by the Holy Spirit, by the spirit of God that has inspired this scripture. For example, the Jewish rabbis long saw in this text a story that's not just a love story but it's a story of the love and the covenant between God and his chosen people. Christian theologians likewise have seen another level, the love between Christ and his Church and some of them have urged that it's the love of God for the individual soul.

These spiritual levels of meaning need not and should not be thought to be something imposed by later readers but rather, in the long standing tradition of interpretation that has been the dominant interpretation prior to the contemporary period. This is the dominant reading. This is layers of meaning that are latent within the text, not because human authors put them there but because of divine inspiration and hence, available for our discovery when we read them prayerfully.

We can also consider, in a second whole genre here, not just wisdom as what God has to teach us, but also what God teaches us a little bit more indirectly by what nature teaches us, what the cosmos teaches us, what all the creatures in the world have to teach us. I think this is a second important sense of wisdom that is contained within the notion of biblical wisdom literature. It's what we can come to understand by looking at what God has made; either the cosmos as a whole or a particular kind of creature and the nature that it has. And then later on, we'll do a special section on human nature.

How many of the proverbs make use of analogies and comparisons with various creatures in order to express their point about human life? This is the application of the knowledge that we do have of nature to questions about human society and human behavior. It's clear that biblical wisdom wants to emphasize this.

While biblical wisdom literature does not offer us a systematic picture of the cosmos or the natures of the various creatures in the way that Greek philosophy, in the way that subsequent sciences have tried to do in the traditions of inquiry that began already in ancient Greece and that have flowered in modern science, nonetheless, there is a deep respect for this type of inquiry within biblical wisdom literature. Think, for example, of the various portraits of Solomon that we encountered, as well as the portraits of the ideal sage in texts like Sirach. They are alluding constantly to the importance of knowledge of the natural world.

Far more prevalent within biblical wisdom literature is knowledge of human nature. Admittedly, when biblical wisdom literature is talking about human nature, it doesn't do it in the abstract patterns of thought that would become typical of Greek philosophy or of other later philosophical traditions, ancient, medieval, and modern, but nonetheless, there is a profound knowledge of human nature. I'd like to call this a third sense of wisdom, namely wisdom as human understanding; wisdom as the knowledge we have of human nature and of human behavior. It's connected to that second sense of wisdom about nature in general, but I think it's really a third and distinct sense because our sphere of human experience is so rich and our need to have a penetrating insight into this is so great.

There is, I think, a third sense then of wisdom as knowledge about human nature in regard to what we can figure out by our reasoning; reasoning on the basis of experience, especially on the experience of how human beings interact and the many ways in which this is taught in the wisdom texts.

The great collection of proverbs that is the book of Proverbs, likewise the collections of proverbs that are in the book of Sirach, strike me as being like this. It seems to me that it is quite right to take these proverbs, not only as formulated under the blessing of divine guidance, but I think it's also important to take them as human wisdom trying to figure out what it is that our experience has meant; what it is that works and what it is that does not work. It's the reason, I think, in which one finds within those collections things that are borrowed from Egypt, things that are borrowed from Mesopotamia. It's a sense that we can embrace as our own human wisdom what others have figured out. Gathered together in books like Proverbs and books like Sirach, these collections of proverbs serve as ways to crystallize the insight and then to convey from one generation to the next, the body of Israel's own received wisdom. If it includes and assimilates the wisdom from other neighboring peoples, so much the better.

There's also the wisdom that comes from questioning. As a philosopher, I just find it so important that we constantly provoke and test with questions to which we don't fully know the answer but we're going to search hard. I see that in biblical wisdom literature too; the way in which pressing these hard questions to the very limit of one's imagination is crucial. The book of Job, for example, strikes me as exemplifying this sense of wisdom in a delightful way. From its opening gambit, it seems to be giving voice to some of the hardest possible sort of questions, such as whether God is just in allowing anyone, and especially someone who is as innocent as Job, to suffer. Likewise, it tries to press the question about whether there must ultimately be some sort of guilt deep down in any case where we find terrible suffering. When we were doing the book of Job, we were plumbing those questions and I think we were showing that the book of Job is designed to show us that the presence of suffering does not mean that there is guilt there, and that we need to relieve people of that burden, and that this too will be wisdom when we figure that out.

It seems to me that these questions that come so readily to the human heart are a deep part of biblical wisdom literature, and that the sapiential literature of the Bible is right to give voice to those questions, and then to debate them in a way that we were trying to show when we put the book of Proverbs up against the book of Job. It's an invitation to us to join the debate because not every line in the Bible can be read as giving us the answer. I think sometimes the lines in the Bible, such as those debates that Job had with his friends, are giving us the question and leading us to the answer. Hence, I would urge that that part of the wisdom literature and that part of wisdom that's involved here, is something to which we are summoned with all of our energy, in that we are really called upon to join the debate.

In trying to do that here in this course, I tried to engage with you and to do it in several ways. For example, I was trying for awhile in some of the lectures on Job, to reuse the parts that C. S. Lewis and other modern authors have done in their reflections. When C. S. Lewis and others come to this question of human suffering, they are really marvelous in that they show us what good reasoning can provide for us here and I think that what they show us is this: that good reasoning requires us to say that God is not being unjust in allowing suffering. The reasoning, as you'll recall from that lecture, is that for God to create creatures that have the power of free choice means that God also creates a world of stable natural laws that govern the interaction, that govern the way, in which objects in the universe deal with one another and that having stable natural laws in which actions have their consequences is the very condition for the possibility of freedom. If there was an immediate correction, if when suffering was about to occur, it was suddenly removed, well, there would no longer be freedom because actions would no longer have their consequences. What figuring that out and what reflecting on that allows us to do is to say that terrible as some sufferings are, the possibility of suffering is simply a concomitant of freedom of choice within the world.

Now, to say that, to give that sort of philosophical explanation that I think is deeply part of the understanding and the interpretation of these biblical texts, to say that is not yet to do everything that we need to do because we need to offer real compassion and real comfort to someone who is in suffering. It's not a matter of just saying nice words. It's a matter of accompanying people who are down in the depths of despair. It's a matter of providing from our resources and from our charity for those who are in need. I have known people that get so mad at God over the fact of suffering, that they reject him. I don't mean that rehearsing the pattern of arguments from C. S. Lewis is going to be a cure-all for that problem. When you're dealing with the person right in your presence, what is needed is real compassion. But I do think that understanding the background here and understanding the way in which freedom does require that there be a situation of natural laws in which suffering is possible, is part of the response that we have to make to the larger situation. And what's most valuable for us is removal of an error of reasoning so that we can be free to reason rightly about the situation and then be ready with a compassionate response.

Providing a compassionate response may well mean readying ourselves to offer personal care, real help to those in suffering. This too is something for which, I think, we need to have practical wisdom. We need the instruction that the books of the biblical wisdom literature tradition provide when we think hard about how best to provide compassion and a true compassion, not a false compassion; about how we should be willing to be generous and charitable in finding the material resources, in finding the right kind of things to say or sometimes—and here I think the biblical wisdom tradition was simply magnificent—in getting us ready for the hard job of simply sitting in compassionate silence, as in the noble tradition of sitting shivah, that I think we saw exemplified in those three friends of Job who sat with him for a full week, simply accompanying him in compassion, when they had nothing particular that they could give him.

Another important part of the problem is the feelings of guilt that can well up in a person. That is, while some people just reject God because of suffering, other people find themselves overwhelmed by guilt, whether in the person's suffering—that was what Job's friends thought Job was undergoing; that he was suffering because of his guilt—or perhaps in simply being close to somebody who's suffering and they wonder whether that person's sinned or whether they themselves did.

Well, just as with the inclination to blame God for allowing suffering, there seems to me to be an error in reasoning here and it was for that reason that I offered, during the part of our lectures that were devoted to the book of Job, I offered at least one attempt to try to clear up the mistake. The relevant point here is this, while actions do have consequences and while freely chosen actions deserve their rewards and punishments, those rewards and punishments need not come about immediately, need not come about directly. They may be deferred for awhile. To think that they do come about immediately all the time is, I think, to make an error and that's the reason why

©2009 The Teaching Company.

Job's friends assumed because he's suffering, he must have been guilty of something.

Rather, I think, it would be much better to say, it would be a truer interpretation and more helpful, to say that God's justice will take care of these things, but that God's justice will take care of these things in his own good time. There are many reasons beyond that, why suffering might come; not all suffering comes as a result of guilt. These reasons include those stable natural laws that we were discussing and the interaction of agents. The reasons include the free decisions of others. When someone who is wicked causes suffering on the part of someone who is innocent, well there we can see what the immediate cause was. It isn't because the innocent was really guilty, it was because of the wickedness of someone who was wicked and it is erroneous to think that all suffering is a payback for guilt. In this, I think that Job's friends simply need to be corrected. What, on the other hand, they should really be praised for is their compassion in sitting shivah and accompanying their friend in those first seven days before they began to speak.

The distinctions that I'm making here, I hope, is clear. Human wisdom, including our little exercise in logic and our reflections on the intrinsic connection between free choices and stable laws of nature, I think that these things can contribute to understanding the problem of suffering; partly by removing erroneous views but also partly by preparing us in character for charity and for compassion. To say that we've removed some of the erroneous views doesn't in any way make the positive contributions of biblical literature any less important or any less relevant. We saw that when we were taking note of the importance of the covenant with Noah and the way in which God revealed that the just and the unjust must live together on this earth, with his promise to shine his sunlight on both, and his promise to send rain on both until the time of final judgment; that he is giving us that time of freedom, the time later to repent of our sins, the time to exhibit the care and compassion, that this is a part of his gift, that there is still time, that there is still opportunity, that there is still freedom.

Let me turn to a different topic, namely, another of the really important aspects of wisdom literature; prayer and reflection. We were noticing, for instance, that there were a number of wisdom psalms and as interludes during our course, from time to time after we finished one of the books, we turned to the Psalter and we tried to consider a number of the psalms that collectively are called the wisdom psalms. These are forms of prayer that are open to the believer and to the one who is still searching, alike. They are ways, I think, to give voice to our need for wisdom about all sorts of things; about the reality of God when we feel in doubt, about the proper conduct of human life when there are mixed motives perhaps, or when there's simply unclarity. And even for wisdom about situations that are just beyond our understanding and that what we have to do is to admit the mystery and to admit the fact that there are limitations on our comprehension.

Happily, the poetry of the Hebrew psalms is not based on rhythm or rhyme, both of which would be hard to translate. Instead, the poetry of the Hebrew psalms is based on balance and on opposition and so these psalms are easily translatable into any language on the earth. I think that's by design. They're a prayer book for religious communities. They're a prayer book for individuals. They're something that believers have close to their heart and perhaps even memorized in some cases.

They're also, I think, wonderful reflections for people who are still searching, because they can be said by people with doubts and with difficulties and with unclarity. They can be said and they can be objects for reflection and for a way to guide one's thinking. On that subject of reflection within prayer, I think we saw some interesting things for instance, in the Wisdom of Solomon. There we met the persona, the figure of King Solomon. And in the process of showing the wisdom for which he is known, it was very significant that while he informs his fellow kings of the earth that his reputation for wisdom is not just the result of his native abilities; he also can direct them to where they must go because it's where he had to go. He asserts that wisdom is a gift he has received, so he reminds his colleagues of the need that he had to pray for that wisdom and then it's not just that he tells them that in the abstract, but that he shows them a way in which to do so. He models it for them.

I think that this is the case for all of us. Whatever our own individual abilities or our accomplishments or our previous experiences, there is a deep need to be receptive of the wisdom if we're going to grow. Part of that receptivity means leaving some time for reflection; finding a time in our schedule. Often what I do is try to plot it out.

What am I going to do tomorrow? And when am I going to leave some space? There is good reason, I think, to follow Solomon's example in raising mind and heart in prayer and asking for wisdom and leaving time for reflection.

Allow me, if you will, just one personal note here at the end of the course. Namely, I want to thank you for joining me on this journey through biblical wisdom literature. It's something that's very, very dear to me. I hope that it's been helpful to you and I wish you many blessings as you continue your journey.

Chronology of Important Figures and Events

Since there is much scholarly debate about the dating of the events in the earlier parts of this timeline, it is impossible to provide specific dates in many cases. This chronology will use the abbreviation "c." (circa) for "about," "fl." (floruit) for designating a date that is likely to have been within the time of the individual's maturity, and "d." for "died." There are many other figures from biblical history who might have been included here. This list concentrates on those who are mentioned in the course of this set of lectures on biblical wisdom literature. It also includes the dates for other figures discussed during these lectures.

Adam and Eve: According to Genesis, the first man and the first woman. Created by God; dates unknown.

Cain and Abel: The first children of Adam and Eve; dates unknown.

Noah: The figure whom God commanded to make the ark in order to survive the flood. Dates unknown.

Abraham: Called by God c. 1850 B.C. to be the father of the chosen people, with his wife Sarah; although they were for long years childless, God gave them a child, Isaac, in their old age.

Isaac: Son of Abraham and Sarah, husband of Rebecca.

Jacob: Twin brother of Esau, son of Isaac and Rebecca, husband of Rachel and Leah. Heir of the promises made to Abraham, progenitor of the 12 tribes of Israel.

Joseph: The 11th son of Jacob; his role in the history of the chosen people is described in Genesis 37–50 (fl. 1650 B.C.).

The slavery of the chosen people in Egypt: The precise dates of the captivity in Egypt are much debated; the period extends from the death of Joseph to the Exodus at the time of Moses.

Moses: Raised up by God to lead the chosen people out of slavery in Egypt (fl. 1250 B.C.).

Exodus: The liberation of the chosen people from Egypt. The date for this event may have been during the reign of Ramses II (1279–1213 B.C.).

***The Instruction of Amen-em-ope* (Egypt)**: A document from the tradition of wisdom literature in Egypt, probably composed c. 1200 B.C.

Saul: The first king of the ancient kingdom of Israel, reigned c. 1047–c. 1007 B.C. (See 1 Samuel 9:1–10:16).

David: The second king of the ancient kingdom of Israel (c. 1037–967 B.C.). He reigned over Judah c. 1007–1000 B.C. and then over Judah and Israel together c. 1000–967 B.C.

Nathan: A prophet at the court of King David (fl. 1000 B.C.).

Solomon: Third king of ancient Israel; born c. 1000 B.C., reigned from c. 971–931 B.C.; builder of the First Temple.

Proverbs: At least some portions of this book seem to come from the time of David and Solomon (10th century B.C.), but the final editing seems to have happened considerably later.

First Temple of Jerusalem: Completed in the 10th century B.C. and destroyed by the Babylonians in 586 B.C.

Rehoboam: Son of Solomon, and thus the third king of the house of David; he ruled over the kingdom of Judah from 931–c. 913 B.C.

Jeroboam: Son of Nebat of Ephraim, ruled over the breakaway Northern Kingdom of Israel c. 931–910 B.C.

Elisha: The disciple of Elijah and his divinely appointed successor as prophet, mid-9th century B.C.

The exile: The 10 northern tribes of Israel went into exile in 721 B.C., and the 2 southern tribes of Judah did so in 587 B.C. The return to Palestine took place in 539 B.C. at the command of King Cyrus of Persia.

Hezekiah: Ruled as King of Judah c. 715–687 B.C.

Josiah: Ruled as King of Judah c. 640–609 B.C.

Book of Job: Perhaps from the 7th century B.C., but the date is disputed. Some date it as early as the time of David and Solomon, but others tend to date it from the time of the exile.

Book of Qoheleth: Although the date of composition is disputed, prevalent scholarly opinion holds that this book was composed sometime after the return from the exile in 539 B.C.

Song of Songs: Also called the Canticle of Canticles; its date of composition is unknown, but it may come from the 5th century B.C.

Joshua: Jewish high priest after the restoration of the temple; reigned c. 516–490 B.C.

Second Temple: The reconstructed Temple at Jerusalem stood from c. 516 B.C. to A.D. 70.

Wisdom of Solomon: A late part of biblical wisdom literature. Very difficult to date; estimates range from 220 B.C. to A.D. 50.

Simon II: Jewish high priest who served from c. 219 to 196 B.C.

Antiochus IV Epiphanes: Seleucid king who lived from c. 215 to 164 B.C.

Sirach: Also called Ben-Sirach or Ecclesiasticus, this book was composed in Hebrew between 200 and 175 B.C. and then translated by the author's grandson into Greek at some point after 132 B.C.

Onias III: A Jewish high priest mentioned in 2 Maccabees (d. 170 B.C.).

King Ptolemy VIII Physikon Euergetes II: He reigned over Egypt from 170 to 163 B.C., then shared rule with his brother Philometor until 145 B.C., and then reigned solely again from 145 to 117 B.C.

Book of Daniel: Composed c. 165 B.C.

Pompey the Great: Roman general, lived 106–48 B.C.

Philo of Alexandria: Great Jewish philosopher and biblical exegete, lived c. 20 B.C.–A.D. 50.

John the Baptist: The cousin of Jesus of Nazareth, lived c. 4 B.C.–A.D. 26.

Jesus of Nazareth: For Christians, the eternal Son of God who became incarnate by taking on human nature as a child in the womb of the Virgin Mary in c. 4 B.C. He was crucified c. A.D. 29. Christians believe that he then rose from the dead and ascended to heaven. The traditional system of dating the years in terms of B.C. and A.D. had regarded the year of his birth as the year 1, but modern investigations into chronology have made it increasingly clear that the 33 years of his life must be dated slightly earlier than the traditional dates.

Destruction of Jerusalem (A.D. 70): The Roman obliteration of the city of Jerusalem and destruction of the temple.

Council of Jamnia (A.D. 90): A gathering of Jewish scholars concerned about the biblical canon.

Marcus Aurelius (A.D. 121–180): Roman emperor and Stoic philosopher, author of Meditations.

Jerome (c. A.D. 347–420): Christian scholar who translated the Bible from Hebrew and Greek into Latin.

Augustine (A.D. 354–430): Christian theologian and bishop of Hippo.

Boethius (c. A.D. 480–524): Roman statesman and philosopher, author of the *Consolation of Philosophy*.

Avicenna (A.D. 980–1037): Islamic philosopher and theologian from Persia.

Maimonides (1135–1204): Medieval Jewish philosopher, author of the *Guide for the Perplexed*.

Averroës (1126–1198): Islamic philosopher from Córdoba, Spain.

Aquinas (1224–1274): Christian philosopher and theologian.

Dante (1265–1321): Author of the *Divine Comedy*.

Ignatius of Loyola (1491–1556): Spiritual writer and founder of the Society of Jesus.

Shakespeare, William (1564–1616): English playwright.

Leibniz, Gottfried Wilhelm (1646–1716): German statesman and philosopher, author of *Theodicy*.

Voltaire (1694–1778): The pen name for François-Marie Arouet, author of *Candide*.

Kant, Immanuel (1724–1804): German philosopher.

Blake, William (1757–1827): Poet and painter whose work includes illustrations of the book of Job.

Newman, John Henry, Cardinal (1801–1890): British theologian, author of "Lead, Kindly Light."

Dickens, Charles (1812–1870): English novelist.

Nietzsche, Friedrich (1844–1900): German philosopher.

Thompson, Francis (1859–1907): British poet, author of the poem "The Hound of Heaven."

Williams, Ralph Vaughan (1872–1958): British composer.

MacLeish, Archibald (1892–1982): American poet.

Hartshorne, Charles (1897–2000): American process philosopher.

Lewis, C. S. (1898–1963): British literary scholar and Christian apologist, author of *The Problem of Pain*.

Wojtyła, Karol (1920–2005): Pope John Paul II.

Glossary

Aaronite priesthood: A line of Jewish priests descended from Aaron, the brother of Moses, charged with various duties related to the offering of sacrifice.

acrostic: A poem structured to have subsequent lines begin with the next letter of the alphabet.

Adonai: A Hebrew term meaning "LORD" that is substituted in the reading of a Hebrew text when the tetragrammaton appears.

alliteration: Repetition of the same consonant sound.

anawim: In Hebrew, "the remnant"—a reference to those left behind in Palestine during the Babylonian captivity.

aphtharsia: The Greek term for "incorruptibility."

apocalyptic: From the Greek term that means "revelation," a genre of biblical writing that often focuses on divine judgment and end times.

apocrypha: A general term used to designate books that are not regarded as part of the biblical canon but nonetheless respected for their antiquity and their connection to a religious tradition. *See also* **deuterocanonical**.

apostles: Those disciples of Jesus whom he appointed as the official witnesses to his resurrection and whom he commissioned to begin spreading the Gospel throughout the world.

Ashkenazic Judaism: A form of Judaism that originated in the Rhineland during the Middle Ages, with distinctive liturgical practices.

assonance: Repetition of the same vowel sound.

athanasia: The Greek term for "immortality."

augury: A practice for trying to determine the future and to ascertain favorable omens, widely practiced in the ancient world but condemned by the Hebrew prophets.

autograph copy: The original manuscript.

Babylonian captivity: The period of exile, beginning in 721 B.C. for the 10 northern tribes of the Kingdom of Israel and in 587 B.C. for the 2 southern tribes of the Kingdom of Judah, that was brought to an end by King Cyrus of Persia in 539 B.C.

Beatitudes: The sayings of Jesus recorded in the Gospels of Matthew (5:3–12) and Luke (6:20–26) that begin "Blessed are …" These sayings are signature aspects of the wisdom of Jesus, but they echo various passages in the Old Testament such as Psalm 37 [36]:11 and Isaiah 61:1–2.

berith: The Hebrew term for "covenant."

Bible: The collection of sacred scriptures. *See also* Hebrew Bible, Old Testament, New Testament, apocrypha, deuterocanonical.

Booths, Feast of: Also called "Feast of Tabernacles." In Hebrew, Sukkoth. The seven-day biblical harvest festival associated with pilgrimage, celebrated beginning the 15th of Tishrei (late September or October). See Leviticus 23:33–43 and John 7:10–26.

canon: The officially recognized collection of sacred books. The term comes from the Greek term *kanon*, which means "rule."

cantillation: Singing and chanting.

catharsis: In Greek, "purification." A term used in literary criticism of Greek tragedy for the cleansing of emotions such as pity and fear brought about in the characters and/or the audience.

Catholic Church: One of the largest Christian communions, comprised of the Western, or Latin, rite (called the Roman Catholic Church) and 22 Eastern Catholic Churches, governed by the Pope, with bishops whose lineage can be traced back to the apostles.

Christ: From the Greek term *christos*, which translates the Hebrew term *messiah*—literally, "the anointed one." A title applied to Jesus of Nazareth, designed to designate him as the one specially anointed by God as the Messiah.

conditional logic: The sort of argumentation that proceeds by the affirmation or denial of some fact to a hypothesis so as to derive a conclusion.

conscience: In general, the power within an individual to reflect and make moral judgments, both retrospectively on prior action and prospectively on actions being considered for the future.

contemplation: A form of mental prayer that often makes use of one's memory and imagination to lift the mind and heart to God.

covenant: A special form of contract or agreement that is made to form a relationship of particularly strong unity and intimacy; the term is used of human marriages as well as of the relationship between God and the chosen people and between Christ and the church.

decalogue: The 10 Commandments given by God to Moses on Mount Sinai, found in Exodus 20:2–17 and Deuteronomy 5:6–21.

deuterocanonical: A technical term that means "second canon" and designates those books regarded as part of the biblical canon by some traditions but as apocryphal by others.

Diaspora: The dispersal of the chosen people to various lands when they were forced to leave Palestine.

diatheke: The Greek term used to translate the Hebrew term *berith*, meaning "covenant."

discernment: The process by which to determine the meaning of a text or an experience.

divination: The practice common in ancient religions for trying to ascertain favorable omens; condemned by the Hebrew prophets.

divine right of kings: A political theory of the early modern period of history by which sovereigns claimed to root their authority in will of God, associated especially with the Stuart and Caroline houses of Great Britain.

dramatic fallacy: When interpreting a literary text, the mistake of simply supposing without sufficient evidence that the words of a fictional character present the author's position on a given issue.

dream vision: An experience of some memorable encounter during sleep, such as those recorded in the book of Daniel.

Dualism: A philosophical approach whose essential feature is recourse to some pair of coprinciples.

Elohim: The most common Hebrew term for "God."

Epicureanism: A school of philosophy originated in Greece by Epicurus that identified pleasure as the goal of life and that made the promotion of pleasure and the reduction of pain the main criterion for decision making, usually with various distinctions between long-term and short-term pleasures, the relative intensity and quality of pleasures, and so on.

epilogue: A section added at the end of a work to bring matters to a conclusion or to offer a reflection on what has taken place.

eschatology: The part of theology devoted to end times, including questions about events to be expected at the conclusion of history and about divine judgment, as well as questions about personal survival after bodily death.

exegete: An interpreter; a commentator on a text.

exhortation: Words of encouragement.

faith: In general, belief; usually said with regard to belief in God and often associated with what is standard belief in a given religious tradition.

fallacy: An error in reasoning.

fatalism: An attitude or belief that one's destiny is fixed in advance.

fear of the LORD: Deep respect for God and an unwillingness to offend the divine will. In biblical wisdom literature, this is called the beginning of wisdom.

Fideism: An approach to life and belief that emphasizes faith over reason. This sometimes includes a suspicion that human reason is incapable of discovering the answer to crucial life questions and an inclination to regard divine revelation alone as sufficient for answering those questions.

genre: Literary type; this term is used to distinguish among various kinds of writing on the basis of literary structure.

goel: A Hebrew term for "redeemer" or "avenger."

Gospel: The term in English for the narratives about the life of Jesus in the New Testament.

Hallel: Literally, "praise," this is the Hebrew word that is usually translated into English as "alleluia."

Hasidim: A Jewish religious movement named from the Hebrew term *hesed*, which means "loving kindness."

hebel: Literally, "breath"; the Hebrew word that is often translated as "vanity."

Hebrew Bible: The set of biblical books written in Hebrew.

hedonist: Pleasure-seeker. Hedonism is a school of philosophy that regards pleasure as the highest good possible for human life.

Hellenization: The process of assimilation to Greek culture.

hokma: The Hebrew term for "wisdom."

Holy Spirit: In Christian usage, the name for the third person of the Holy Trinity.

Holy Trinity: A term in Christian usage to designate the mystery of there being three persons in one God (Father, Son or Word, and Holy Spirit).

immanent eschatology: A theological view that emphasizes this world rather than some other (postmortal) world as the place where God's plan will be realized.

immortality: Literally, deathlessness; usually said of the soul, to indicate ongoing personal survival after bodily death.

incarnation: Literally, the taking on of flesh. It is the term in Christian usage for the assumption of a human nature by the second person of the Holy Trinity; the conception of Jesus in the womb of Mary is often described as "the incarnation of the Word."

incorruptibility: The state of being unable to be corrupted or destroyed; usually said of the body after resurrection from the dead.

kingdom of God/kingdom of heaven: Terms especially associated with the preaching of Jesus to designate the new age that his coming was designed to bring about.

kyrios: Greek term for "LORD."

lev: Hebrew term for "heart."

Levite: A member of the Hebrew tribe of Levi, charged with certain religious duties, including the singing of psalms during temple services as well as various construction and maintenance tasks in the temple.

liturgy of the hours: In Christian usage, the official order of prayers to be offered at various times during each day, consisting primarily of psalms and supplemented by various hymns, readings from scripture, and other prayers.

Logos: A Greek term with many interrelated meanings, often used in the New Testament as "Word" to designate the second person of the Holy Trinity.

mashal: The Hebrew term for a parable or riddle.

meden agan: Literally, "nothing too much"; a phrase from Greek ethics used to express the idea that virtue consists in moderation.

meditation: A form of mental prayer that often involves thinking about the meaning of a scriptural text and generating a personal response.

Messiah: From the Hebrew word for "anointed one," a term used to designate someone specially appointed by God and anointed for a sacred purpose. The Greek translation of this term is *christos*, from which we get the word "Christ" in English. In Christian usage, this term refers especially to Jesus as the one anointed by God to carry out the work of redemption.

midrash: In Hebrew, "study." The term refers especially to a certain form of biblical interpretation often used for homiletic purposes.

Mizrahic Judaism: A form of Judaism originating in the Middle East, with a distinctive form of liturgical practice.

nephesh: In Hebrew, "a living being"—often translated as "soul."

New Testament: The Christian name for the part of the Bible that was written after Christ's coming. Since the term "testament" means "covenant," the term is intended to suggest that Christ established the new covenant prophesied in Jeremiah 31:31.

non multa, sed multum: Literally, "not many things, but much"; a Latin-language saying to express the idea that it is better to focus more deeply on a few things than widely on many things in a superficial way.

Old Testament: The Christian name for the part of the Bible that was written prior to the coming of Christ. The term "testament" is the English translation of the words in Hebrew, Latin, and Greek that mean "covenant."

omnipotent: All-powerful; this is often listed as an attribute of God.

omniscient: All-knowing; this is often listed as an attribute of God.

original sin: In Christian usage, the name for the sin of Adam and Eve that resulted in their being cast out of the Garden of Eden; this is sometimes called "the Fall." The term also refers to the wounded state of human nature inherited by all human beings subsequent to Adam and Eve.

Orthodox Church: One of the largest Christian communions in the world, composed of numerous autocephalous (self-ruled) ecclesial bodies, with bishops whose lineage can be traced back to the apostles.

parable: A short, succinct story used to illustrate some moral or religious teaching.

paradox: An apparent contradiction.

Passover: The Jewish feast commemorating God's deliverance of Israel from slavery in Egypt.

Pentateuch: A term used for the first five books of the Bible: Genesis, Exodus, Leviticus, Numbers, and Deuteronomy.

political philosophy: The branch of philosophy concerned with theories of civil governance and social organization.

prayer: Some form of raising the mind and heart to God. Prayer can take many forms, including the use of set texts and community rituals as well as meditation, contemplation, and spontaneous expressions.

process philosophy/theology: A school of thought that emphasizes change and experience over form and substance in its general account of the universe; its typical approach to theodicy tends to deny the omnipotence and/or the omniscience of God.

Protestantism: A general term for various forms of Christian faith and practice that have had their origin during or since the Reformation of the 16th century.

proverb: A pithy, memorable saying; a maxim.

Psalter: The collection of psalms.

psalterion: The stringed instrument used to accompany the psalms.

purgatory: In Christian usage, a term to designate the place and the process of the soul's purification from sin and vice, in preparation for union with God in heaven.

qahal: Literally "assembly," it is the Hebrew word at the base of the title of the book Qoheleth, which is often translated as "The Preacher" (in Greek, Ecclesiastes).

Rabbinic Judaism: The mainstream system of Judaism after the Diaspora, once the Roman destruction of the Second Temple made it impossible to practice the religious customs and animal sacrifices prescribed for worship in the temple.

resurrection of the body: The restoration of a body to life at some point after bodily death. *See also* **immorality**, **incorruptibility**.

righteousness: A theological term for the rectitude of a person's life and actions when judged to be holy and pleasing to God.

Rosh Hashanah: The Hebrew term for "new year"; see Leviticus 23:24 and Ezekiel 40:1.

ruah: In Hebrew, "breath" or "spirit"; often translated as "soul."

sage: A person of wisdom.

sapiential: Wise; from *sapientia*, the Latin term for wisdom.

Satan: In Hebrew, "accuser." In the books of Job and Zechariah, one who challenged God. In Christian and Muslim usage, a rebellious or fallen angel; a demon.

Sephardic Judaism: A form of Judaism that originated in the Iberian Peninsula (modern Spain) and has a distinctive form of liturgical practices.

Septuagint: The Greek translation of the Hebrew Bible.

Shaddai **(or** *El Shaddai***)**: A name for God in Hebrew, meaning "God Almighty."

Sheol: The Hebrew term for the abode of the dead, the underworld. By the 2nd century B.C., it was also the name for those awaiting the resurrection of the dead or confined to torment after death as the punishment for their sins.

shivah: In Judaism, a bereavement practice that consists of a week-long period of grief and mourning that immediately follows a burial.

skepticism: A philosophical attitude of doubt, either in general about the possibility of knowledge or in particular about specific knowledge claims.

soliloquy: A relatively lengthy speech by one individual, addressed to the audience or reader rather than to some other character.

soul, spirit: Terms used to refer to what makes someone alive. These terms are used in various ways, including as a center of personal consciousness during life and as the seat of personal existence beyond death.

Stoicism: A philosophical school of thought known for its rigorous mental discipline and for its cultivation of an attitude of indifference to whatever is outside of human control.

Sukkoth: *See* **Booths, Feast of**.

suzerainty treaty: A technical term for a typical form of contractual association in the ancient Near East between a superior and an inferior.

synoptic: A term used to group together the gospels of Matthew, Mark, and Luke, which tend to have relatively close parallels in their presentation of the narrative of the life of Jesus.

Talmud: The central text of Rabbinical Judaism that records discussions on Jewish law, customs, history, and ethics. It consists of the Mishnah (the written account of Judaism's oral law) and the Gemara (a later record of discussions about the Mishnah and the TaNaK).

TaNaK: A Hebrew acronym used to identify the three parts of the Bible: *Torah*, *N'viim* (Prophets), and *Ktuvim* (Writings).

tehillim: Literally, "hymns of praise"; the Hebrew word for the Psalms.

testamentum: The Latin term for "covenant."

tetragrammaton: Literally, "the four-lettered word" when referring to the sacred name of God revealed to Moses that (out of respect) should not be pronounced: YHWH. When it occurs in a Hebrew text, the word *Adonai* (LORD) is to be pronounced instead.

theodicy: A generic name for philosophical efforts to justify the ways of God, especially in light of suffering.

theophany: A divine appearance, such as the manifestation of God on Mount Sinai.

Torah: A term of Hebrew origin for "law" that refers, in the narrowest sense, to the Decalogue, but more broadly to the books of the Bible that focus on the law: Exodus, Leviticus, Numbers, and Deuteronomy.

Typikon: A liturgical book containing instructions about the order of church services, used by various Eastern Orthodox and Eastern Catholic churches.

Vulgate: Saint Jerome's Latin translation of the Bible.

wisdom: In general, a term for expressing excellence in knowledge, understanding, experience, judgment, and insight. In the Bible, the term is used especially for the divine gift of such excellence but also for human efforts to achieve such excellence. The term is also used in a personified way in the various wisdom poems and in the first nine chapters of Proverbs.

wisdom poem: A term for grouping together special passages in biblical wisdom literature such as Proverbs 8, Job 28, and Sirach 24, in which the figure of Wisdom is predominant.

wisdom psalm: A term used to group together a number of psalms marked by the typical themes of biblical wisdom literature.

yad (**pl.** *yamin*): In Hebrew, "hand(s)."

Yom Kippur: In Jewish practice, the Day of Atonement—marked by fasting, prayer, and repentance. See Leviticus 23:27.

Bibliography

Axel, Gabriel. *Babette's Feast*. VHS. Santa Monica, CA: Metro Goldwyn Mayer, 2001. A video recording of the film produced by Just Betzer and Bo Christensen.

Becker, Ernest. *The Denial of Death*. New York: Free Press, 1973. A philosopher's reflections on the problem of death and immortality.

Benedict XVI. *Jesus of Nazareth*. Translated by Adrian J. Walker. New York: Doubleday, 2007. Much fine reflection on the wisdom of Jesus. See especially chapter 7, "The Message of the Parables," pages 183–217.

Blake, William. *Illustrations of the Book of Job*. Edited by Malcolm Cormack. Richmond, VA: Virginia Museum of Fine Arts, 1997. A lovely volume of Blake's illustrations, with helpful commentary.

Bloch, Ariel, and Chana Bloch. *The Song of Songs: The World's First Great Love Poem*. New York: Random House, 2006. A literary appreciation of the Song of Songs from a Jewish perspective.

Boadt, Lawrence. *Reading the Old Testament: An Introduction*. New York: Paulist Press, 1984. An excellent introduction to the Bible, written from a Christian perspective.

Boethius, Anicius Manlius Severinus. *Consolation of Philosophy*. Translated by H. R. James. New York: Barnes & Noble, 2005. An English translation of a classical work by an early Christian philosopher.

Browne, Neil, and Stuart Keely. *Asking the Right Questions: A Guide to Critical Thinking*. Upper Saddle River, NJ: Prentice Hall, 2006. A college-level logic text.

Christianson, Eric S. *Ecclesiastes through the Centuries*. Malden, MA: Blackwell, 2007. A scholarly study on the use and interpretation of the book Qoheleth.

Clifford, Richard J. *Deuteronomy, with an Excursus on Covenant and Law*. Wilmington, DE: Michael Glazier, 1982. Particularly helpful for its presentation of the idea of covenant.

———. *Proverbs: A Commentary*. Louisville, KY: Westminster John Knox Press, 1999. A scholarly commentary on the book of Proverbs.

———. *The Wisdom Literature*. Nashville, TN: Abingdon Press, 1998. A scholarly study of each of the books of sapiential literature.

————, ed. *Wisdom Literature in Mesopotamia and Israel*. Leiden, Netherlands: Brill, 2007. A scholarly study of biblical wisdom literature and some of its ancient sources.

Collins, John J. *Daniel: A Commentary on the Book of Daniel*. Minneapolis, MN: Fortress, 1993. A scholarly commentary.

————. *Jewish Wisdom in the Hellenistic Age*. Louisville, KY: Westminster Press, 1997. A scholarly study of biblical wisdom literature with emphasis on the Hellenistic period.

Da Palestrina, Giovanni Pierluigi. *Motets*. Orleans, MA: Paraclete Press, 1999. Compact disc. A fine recording of two of Palestrina's Masses and six other motets.

Davies, Philip R. *Daniel*. Sheffield, UK: JSOT, 1985. A scholarly commentary.

De Lubac, Henri. *Medieval Exegesis: The Four Senses of Scripture*. Translated by Marc Sebanc and E. Macierowski. 2 vols. Grand Rapids, MI: Eerdmans, 1998. A scholarly study of biblical exegesis in the Middle Ages, from a Christian viewpoint.

Dell, Katherine. *"Get Wisdom, Get Insight": An Introduction to Israel's Wisdom Literature*. London: Darton, 2002. An introductory account of sapiential literature.

————. *Shaking a Fist at God: Understanding Suffering through the Book of Job*. London: Fount, 1995. A contemporary theologian's reflections on Job and the problem of theodicy.

DiLella, Alexander. "Sirach." In *New Jerome Biblical Commentary*. Edited by Raymond E. Brown, Joseph A. Fitzmyer, and Roland E. Murphy, 496–509. Upper Saddle River, NJ: Prentice Hall, 1989. A fine overview of the book of Sirach as well as rather pointed commentary, verse-by-verse.

Dodd, C. H. *The Parables of the Kingdom*. Glasgow, Scotland: Fount, 1978. Originally published 1961 by Scribner. A scholarly study of the parables found in the Gospels.

Donin, Hayim Halevy. *To Pray as a Jew: A Guide to the Prayer Book and the Synagogue Service*. New York: Basic Books, 1980. A popularly written account of Jewish styles of prayer.

Duggan, Michael. *The Consuming Fire: A Christian Introduction to the Old Testament*. San Francisco, CA: Ignatius Press, 1991. The material on pages 393–499 deals with biblical wisdom literature in general.

Dumbrell, William J. *Covenant and Creation: A Theology of the Old Testament Covenants*. Carlisle, PA: Paternoster Press, 1997. A popularly written account of covenant theology.

Elbogen, Ismar. *Jewish Liturgy: A Comprehensive History*. Translated by Raymond P. Scheindlin. Philadelphia, PA: Jewish Publication Society, 1993. A scholarly study.

Estes, Daniel J. *Handbook on the Wisdom Literature and Psalms*. Grand Rapids, MI: Baker Academic, 2005. A scholarly account of the breadth of biblical wisdom literature.

Gallagher, Timothy M. *The Discernment of Spirits: An Ignatian Guide for Everyday Living*. New York: Crossroad, 2005. A commentary on the rules for the discernment of spirits devised by Ignatius of Loyola, with many practical examples.

———. *Spiritual Consolation: An Ignatian Guide for the Greater Discernment of Spirits*. New York: Crossroad, 2007. A highly accessible guidebook on spiritual direction.

Garrett, Duane. *Song of Songs/Lamentation*s. Nashville, TN: Thomas Nelson, 2004. A detailed commentary on Song of Songs and on Lamentations, with attention to literary and theological topics.

Glatzer, Nahum, ed. *The Dimensions of Job*. New York: Schocken, 1969. A collection of essays on the book of Job.

Goldingay, John. *Daniel*. Dallas, TX: Word Books, 1989. A scholarly commentary.

Graver, Margaret. *Stoicism and Emotion*. Chicago: University of Chicago Press, 2007. A scholarly study of Stoic philosophy.

Habel, Norman. *The Book of Job*. Philadelphia, PA: Westminster, 1985. A literary reading of Job.

Hartshorne, Charles. *Omnipotence and Other Theological Mistakes*. Albany, NY: SUNY Press, 1984. An account of the problem of theodicy from the perspective of process thought.

Hillers, Delbert R. *Covenant: The History of a Biblical Idea*. Baltimore, MD: The Johns Hopkins University Press, 1969. A scholarly account of the biblical notion of covenant.

Jenson, Robert W. *Song of Songs*. Presbyterian, 2005. A fine commentary on Song of Songs with good attention to the various levels of scriptural meaning.

Jeremias, Joachim. *The Parables of Jesus*. 2nd rev. ed. Translated by S. H. Hooke. New York: Scribner, 1972. A scholarly study of the parables found in the Gospels.

John Paul II. *On the Christian Meaning of Human Suffering*. Boston: Pauline Books, 2005. An English translation of the 1984 papal letter *Salvifici Doloris* on the problems of suffering and theodicy. It includes considerable reflection on the book of Job and the life of Jesus.

Kirzner, Yitchok. *Making Sense of Suffering: A Jewish Approach*. Brooklyn, NY: Mesorah, 2002. A book on the problems of suffering and theodicy in response to Kushner.

Kolarcik, Michael. *The Ambiguity of Death in the Book of Wisdom 1–6: A Study of Literary Structure and Interpretation*. Rome: Pontifical Biblical Institute, 1991. A scholarly study on the first third of Wisdom of Solomon.

Kreeft, Peter. *Three Philosophies of Life*. San Francisco, CA: Ignatius Press, 1990. A Christian philosopher's treatment of the books of Job, Qoheleth, and Song of Songs.

Krüger, Thomas. *Qoheleth: A Commentary*. Translated by O. C. Dean Jr. Minneapolis, MN: Fortress Press, 2004. A scholarly commentary.

Kushner, Harold S. *When Bad Things Happen to Good People*. New York: Knopf, 2004. A popular book about the problems of human suffering and theodicy.

Leaney, A. R. C. *The Jewish and Christian World 200 B.C. to A.D. 200*. New York: Cambridge University Press, 1984. A detailed account of the religious history of Judaism and early Christianity.

Leibniz, Gottfried Wilhelm. *Theodicy*. Translated by Austin M. Farrer. LaSalle, IL: Open Court, 1985. A famous approach to the theodicy problem.

Levenson, Jon D. *Sinai and Zion: An Entry into the Jewish Bible*. Minneapolis, MN: Winston Press, 1985. A scholarly introduction to the notions of Torah and covenant.

Lewis, C. S. *The Problem of Pain*. New York: HarperCollins, 2001. A philosophical and theological approach to the problem of theodicy from a Christian viewpoint.

————. *Reflections on the Psalms*. London: Geoffrey Bless, 1958. A consideration of the meaning of various psalms, from a Christian viewpoint.

Lienhard, Joseph T. *The Bible, the Church, and Authority: The Canon of the Christian Bible in History and Theology*. Collegeville, MN: Liturgical Press, 1995. An historical study of the topic of the biblical canon.

Long, George, trans. *The Meditations of Marcus Aurelius: Spiritual Teachings and Reflections*. London: Duncan Baird, 2006. A translation of a classic spiritual work by a Stoic philosopher.

MacLeish, Archibald. *J. B.: A Play in Verse*. Boston: Houghton Mifflin, 1986. A contemporary play on the theme of Job.

Merton, Thomas. *Bread in the Wilderness*. New York: New Directions, 1997. A reissue of Merton's 1953 classic book on praying the Psalms.

Mowinckel, Sigmund. *The Psalms in Israel's Worship*. Grand Rapids, MI: Eerdmans, 2004. A historical account of how the Psalms have been used in Jewish liturgy.

Murphy, Roland E. *Ecclesiastes*. Dallas, TX: Word, 1992. A scholarly commentary.

————, trans. *Proverbs*. Nashville, TN: Nelson, 1998. Includes translator's commentary. Especially helpful for its detailed analysis of the wisdom poem in chapter 8 and the poem on the ideal spouse in chapter 31.

————. *The Song of Songs: A Commentary on the Book of Canticles or the Song of Songs*. Minneapolis, MN: Augsburg Fortress Press, 1990. An extensive account of the historical context and theological understandings of the Song of Songs.

————. *The Tree of Life: An Exploration of Biblical Wisdom Literature*. 3rd ed. Grand Rapids, MI: Eerdmans, 2002. A fine account of biblical wisdom literature that provides helpful access to the technical scholarship.

Neusner, Jacob. *A Rabbi Talks with Jesus*. Rev. ed. Montreal, QC: McGill-Queen's University Press, 2000. A Jewish reflection on the person and wisdom of Jesus.

Neusner, Jacob, and Noam M. M. Neusner, eds. *The Book of Jewish Wisdom: The Talmud of the Well-Considered Life*. New York: Continuum, 1996. An anthology of Jewish wisdom texts.

Newman, John Henry. "Lead, Kindly Light." In *Oxford Book of English Mystical Verse*. Oxford: Clarendon Press, 1917. A poem with great significance about the problems of suffering and wisdom.

Nickelsburg, George W. E. *Resurrection, Immortality, and Eternal Life in Intertestamental Judaism and Early Christianity*. Cambridge, MA: Harvard University Press, 2006. A scholarly study on the topic of immortality and resurrection, especially with reference to Wisdom of Solomon.

Perdue, Leo, and W. Clark Gilpin. *The Voice from the Whirlwind: Interpreting the Book of Job*. Nashville, TN: Abingdon Press, 1992. A theological reflection on the book of Job.

Pinckaers, Servais. *The Sources of Christian Ethics*. Washington, DC: The Catholic University of America Press, 1995. A wonderful account of Christian moral theology, especially good on the Beatitudes.

Pope, Marvin H. *Song of Songs*. New York: Doubleday, 1995. A scholarly study of the background, content, and applications of Song of Songs.

Pritchard, James B., ed. *Ancient Near Eastern Texts Relating to the Old Testament*. 3rd ed. with supplement. Princeton, NJ: Princeton University Press, 1969. A scholarly collection of the ancient source texts for biblical wisdom literature.

Sanders, Jack T. *Ben Sira and Demotic Wisdom*. Atlanta, GA: Society of Biblical Literature, 1983. An account of the theology of the book of Sirach in relation to other wisdom traditions.

Scott, R. B. Y., ed. and trans. *The Anchor Bible: Proverbs, Ecclesiastes*. Garden City, NY: Doubleday, 1965. A scholarly commentary with translation.

Seow, C. L. *The Anchor Bible: Ecclesiastes; A New Translation with Introduction and Commentary*. New York: Doubleday, 1997. A scholarly commentary on Qoheleth.

Simpson, William Wynn. *Jewish Prayer and Worship*. London: SCM Press, 1965. An introductory account, designed to introduce Christians to the subject of Jewish worship.

Skehan, Patrick W., and Alexander A. DiLella. *The Anchor Bible: The Wisdom of Ben Sira*. New York: Doubleday, 1989. A scholarly commentary.

Thomson, Francis. "Hound of Heaven." In *Oxford Book of English Mystical Verse*. New York: Acropolis Books, 1997. A poem of great spiritual depth on God's interest in each person.

Tournay, Raymond J. *Seeing and Hearing God with the Psalms: The Prophetic Liturgy of the Second Temple in Jerusalem*. Translated by J. Edward Crowley. Sheffield, UK: JSOT Press, 1991. A scholarly account of historical practice of Jewish liturgy.

U.S. Catholic Church. *Catechism of the Catholic Church*. New York: Doubleday, 1995. An official text on Catholic teachings in the form of a catechism. Especially part 4, "Christian Prayer."

Von Rad, Gerhard. *Wisdom in Israel*. Nashville, TN: Abingdon Press, 1972. A scholarly study of sapiential literature by an eminent Jewish authority.

Whybray, R. N. *Ecclesiastes*. Grand Rapids, MI: Eerdmans, 1989. A scholarly commentary.

———. "The Wisdom Psalms." In *Wisdom in Ancient Israel*. Edited by John Day, Robert P. Gordon, and H. G. M. Williamson, 152–160. Cambridge: Cambridge University Press, 1995. An article on the set of psalms that have special relevance to biblical wisdom literature.

Wiesenthal, Simon. *The Sunflower*. New York: Schocken Books, 1997. A story about Wiesenthal's own experiences in a concentration camp that brings out the problem of undeserved suffering.

Williams, Ralph Vaughan. *Job: A Masque for Dancing*. English Northern Philharmonia, conducted by David-Lloyd Jones. Naxos Music Library, 1997. Compact disc. A presentation of the story of Job in music and dance, based on the illustrations to Job created by William Blake.

Winston, David. *The Anchor Bible: The Wisdom of Solomon; A New Translation with Introduction and Commentary*. Garden City, NY: Doubleday, 1979. A scholarly commentary.

Witherington, Ben. *Jesus the Sage: The Pilgrimage of Wisdom*. Minneapolis, MN: Fortress Press, 1994. A scholarly study.

Wojtyła, Karol (later, Pope John Paul II). *Job*. In *The Collected Plays and Writings on Theater*. Translated by Boleslaw Taborski. Berkeley: University of California Press, 1987. A contemporary drama on the theme of Job.

Zuck, Roy B., ed. *Sitting with Job: Selected Studies on the Book of Job*. Eugene, OR: WIPF & Stock, 2003. A collection of essays on the book of Job.

Biblical Translations Cited in This Course:

The Apocryphal New Testament. Translated by Montague Rhodes James. Oxford: Clarendon Press, 1969.

The Holy Bible: Revised Standard Version Containing the Old and New Testaments and the Apocrypha. London and New York: Thomas Nelson and Sons, 1959.

The Jerusalem Bible. Garden City, NY: Doubleday, 1966.

The New American Bible. Edited by Donald Senior. New York and Oxford: Oxford University Press, 1990.

New King James Version of the Bible. London: Hodder & Stoughton, 1994.

The Psalms: A New Translation. London: The Grail, 1963. Translated from the Hebrew and arranged for singing to the psalmody of Joseph Gelineau.

Zondervan New International Version Study Bible. General editor, Kenneth L. Barker. Grand Rapids, MI: Zondervan, 2002.

Notes

Notes